'Cos we only know,
That's there's gonna be a show
When the Everton boys are there.

'It's a Grand Old Team'
(Traditional song, adapted by Everton fans)

Prologue

SINCE I could first walk – and often when I couldn't – I have been an Everton fan. Don't laugh. We used to be good. Very good. I've seen them win the First Division more than once. I've seen them win the FA Cup a few times too and the old European Cup Winners' Cup. No one can deny we have a fantastic history. But therein lies the problem.

As with most football clubs, we sing songs – awful, cheesy anthems. You'd think the city that spawned the Beatles could come up with better compositions. The same song from which the title of this book is taken begins with the bold statement: 'It's a grand old team to play for, it's a grand old team to support, and if you know your history, it's enough to make your heart go woo woo woo woo woo!' And it's true. Our history, some of which I'll proudly recall in the following pages, is a great one. Our problem is that what's been happening at Goodison in recent years certainly doesn't make my heart go 'woo woo woo woo woo'. Whatever the opposite of 'woo woo woo woo woo' is, my heart has been doing that. So, what went wrong?

We were one of the most successful clubs of the 1980s. In May 1987 we had won our second league title in three years and should have enjoyed a fruitful campaign in Europe. We were set to enter the 1990s as one of the most successful clubs in Europe, with a full trophy room and enough money and prestige to attract the best footballers, but the European success that was within our grasp – and the resulting income that would have powered the club into the Premier League – didn't happen. Instead, the victory we tasted in 1987 turned sour as soon as the final whistle had been blown and we had lifted the First Division trophy because we knew we would not be taking part in the following season's most elite European club football tournament. In the wake of the terrible events at Heysel for the 1985 European Cup Final between Liverpool and Juventus, every English club had been banned from European competition for six years. That meant whoever topped the First Division would not enjoy the benefits of a lucrative run in the European Cup. And in 1987 that club was Everton. It felt very unfair at the time, and the irony that it was due to the reckless behaviour of a small band of moronic Liverpool fans was not lost on Evertonians. It was a very dramatic episode in the long-running soap opera involving the City's two football clubs.

Our long slow slide into mediocrity during the 1990s was halted in 2004 when Bill Kenwright took over the club and appointed David Moyes for a period of relative success before we were bought by Farad Moshiri – close friend of Alisher Usmanov, often described as a 'leading Russian businessman' and close friend of Vladimir Putin, which he denies. It transpired that Moshiri's poor judgement in choosing friends was dwarfed by his catastrophic lack of judgement as the owner of a football club. He spent hundreds of millions taking us to the brink of disaster and nearly ended our proud record of having one of the longest stays in the top flight of English football.

But we now have new American owners, The Friedkin Group, and hope has returned to the Blue side of the city. Hope, though, is the fickle companion of every football fan. In the film *Clockwise* John Cleese plays a headmaster trying to get to a conference but being thwarted every step of the way. Pushed to the limits, he finally breaks down and cries out: 'It's not the despair. I can take the despair. It's the hope I can't stand.' Yet for a football fan, hope is often the only straw we can grasp – hope that next time it will be different. I am never more hopeful than during the short walk up the hill from my childhood home to Goodison Park hours before a ball has been kicked. At that point in the afternoon the score is still 0-0 and there's all to play for. OK, so we might be playing Manchester City in about an hour, and we haven't won a game in five weeks, and most of our defence is injured, but what if...? Yes, it's the hope that kills. Nevertheless, here's hoping the Friedkins can pull us out of this nosedive.

This book is, above all else, a love letter to my football club – one of the longest relationships of my life. (As with any long relationship, this one has had its challenges, and I must admit that I haven't always behaved well.) I'll recount the great victories, the heart-breaking defeats and the some of the controversies off the pitch but, as I began to think about the story this book will tell, I realised that my lifelong and sometimes long-distance relationship with Everton runs much deeper than the reportage of footballing matters. And so this is not only a book about football. The story of my relationship with Everton is also the story of my relationship with my family and with the great city of Liverpool itself, my home. In fact, it would be fair to say that it was Everton that provided me with a way to come back to a family and to a home that, for several reasons, I tried to run away from many years before. This book is about how the love for a football team can bring a prodigal son home, back to the city and family he never stopped loving even if he sometimes struggled to admit it, let alone show it. And for that I am truly grateful to you, Everton FC.

1

Goodbye, Goodison

LIFE IS filled with 'last times' – moments we say goodbye to people or things we took for granted – and, for the most part, in that moment we have no idea that the last time is happening, that this is the 'last time'. I can't remember the last time I carried each of my children to bed. I can't remember the last time I spoke to my father before he died suddenly. I can't remember the last time I said goodbye to the many things I've taken for granted in my life. But today is different. Today I know: THIS IS THE LAST TIME.

The date is 18 May 2025. The venue, Goodison Park. The match, Everton v Southampton. On paper it's a game of little consequence. Everton are safe in thirteenth place in the Premier League while Southampton are returning to the Championship after a chastening season in the top flight. But today is not about those ninety minutes. It is about the last 130 years. Everton FC have played football at Goodison Park since 1892, a total of 133 years, and I have been coming here for nearly half that time – since 1959, when I was four years old.

Goodison is situated in a maze of narrow streets in Walton, where I spent the first nineteen years of my life. Our house is a ten-minute walk up Walton Lane, and I have made that trip hundreds of times: first with my father, then, after my father's death in 1978, with my uncle and stepfather, and now with my three sons. But today is the last time I'll come here to watch eleven young men in blue run around kicking a ball to the delight and sometimes dismay of thirty-nine thousand devoted fans. Technically it won't be the last time football is staged here. The good news is Everton's women are taking possession of the ground to make it their new home, so it will live on as a football venue and not be turned into an Asda. But this is the last time I will sit in the seat I've sat in for nearly thirty years and go through the range of feelings that only watching your football team can produce.

It's a sunny day and the crowds have surrounded the stadium since 8 a.m. The kick-off is stupidly early, at noon, but we arrived at 9.25 a.m. My company, Hat Trick Productions, is sponsoring this game. It has sponsored Everton games for about twenty-five years. I think it's important for a small business to extend its relationships with its suppliers and customers with corporate entertaining. For some it's a night at the opera, for others a day at a Lord's Test, and for Hat Trick it's a 200-mile trip to Goodison every year. The fact I am a lifelong Everton fan is purely coincidental, you understand.

So here I am with my three sons, Joe, George and Jack. With us is my uncle Gerard, now 88 – my father's younger brother and the last surviving sibling of a family of nine, every one of them a Blue. My brother John is also here, although he's a Red. We don't shout about it, but he wanted to come I think because his father – also called John, my stepfather, an Everto-nian – had sat next to me and Uncle Gerard for nearly twenty years before his death ten years ago.

My regular season tickets are situated just behind where the sponsors sit, so if I turn around I can see easily Debbie and her family, next to whom we've sat for many years through the high and lows of being a football fan. We aren't close friends, but we have shared

decades of watching our team together. We've sponta-
neously hugged on the odd occasion when a goal has
been scored, and we've cheered together and booed
together. Together we have suffered the last ten years
of steady decline. We are bonded. And we all know
this is the last time we'll do this together. We'll all be
saying goodbye at the end of today and probably won't
be sitting next to each other in the new stadium. There
is a sadness among us but it's bathed in warmth. We've
all had a good time but now this part is over. This is it:
goodbye, Goodison.

The match comes and goes, and we win 2-0. We don't
need the points to stay up, which is a bit of a novelty of
late. Last season we left it until the last game; the season
before wasn't much better. But today isn't just about the
football. It's about the Big Goodbye. We've been told
there will be a post-match celebration to mark this
moment in the club's history. But what will it be?

After the final whistle, over the PA system the club's
announcer asks us to go off for fifteen minutes and
have a drink. We can, he says, bring our drinks back in.
Drinks are not usually allowed inside the stadium but
today is an exception. An appreciative murmur ripples
through the crowd. A first on the last day. What have

they got up their sleeve? Rumours start to circulate. 'I've heard that Paul McCartney is going to give a post-match concert. He's a Blue, after all,' someone opines. Yeah, sure. 'John Lennon is more likely to turn up.'

We traipse back in, some clutching half-drunk pints of lager, others with Guinness; someone trots out with a bottle of wine and glasses like they're going to a garden party. It seems weirdly out of place. We take our seats and look down on a transformed pitch. Not twenty minutes ago it was a playing field with twenty-two young men running around kicking a ball and occasionally each other, but now it is a very different place. Three stages have been strategically erected, one in each penalty area and the other in the centre circle. In front of these stages are rows of shining white chairs, the kind you see at outdoor weddings in Ben Stiller movies. It all looks so neat and sweet and posh, like we've all been invited to a royal garden party. Maybe the twat with the bottle of wine has got it right.

The excitement is now mounting. What has the club planned for us? To be honest, given their recent track record on the pitch, some of us have low expectations. Then the PA system blares out the familiar klaxon sound that usually announces the arrival of the teams onto the pitch, but now it's to get our attention. A lone female violinist takes to the stage in front of the Stanley Park End. The crowd of forty thousand people falls silent. Perfect silence from one of the noisiest crowds in football is deafening. There's usually some idiot who can't bear the silence and shouts out. Not this time; no one says a word. We're at a funeral, here to pay our respects. There is no going back. We really are saying goodbye to our football home, this place where I've been coming for sixty-five years. We can all feel it, and then the violinist takes her bow and begins to play. It's slow and beautiful and immediately familiar: it's the 'Theme from Z Cars', which has welcomed Everton onto the pitch at every home game since the 1960s. It's a brilliant touch. To turn the melody we've all heard thousands of times amid cheers and loud applause as an anthem of welcome and anticipation into a sad, elegiac lament of farewell is just genius. I think, *I'm going to be a mess by the end of this*. The violinist finishes and the crowd erupts. How will they top this?

'Goodison Park', the club's announcer bellows, 'now please welcome your host for the End of an Era celebrations…' Was this the Paul McCartney moment? No, it's: '…Gethin Jones!'

Don't worry, I didn't know who he was either. Gethin, it turns out, is a friendly Welshman who gushes the ready-made exuberance of the practised television presenter – which, according to someone nearby, is exactly what he is. Gethin tells us that, as a lifelong Evertonian, it's an absolute thrill for him to be here at Goodison. 'He used to present *Blue Peter*,' a know-all in our group informs us. We nod solemnly; that figures.

Drawing on his *Blue Peter* experience, Gethin keeps things moving and tells the crowd that we are now going to welcome onto the hallowed ground the heroes from yesteryear, first from the 1960s and 70s... The crowd begins to cheer and onto the pitch walk – in some cases very gingerly – a group of men now in their seventies and eighties, men whom as a young boy I watched race around this pitch scoring goals, making tackles, saving penalties, hearing their name on the lips of thousands of fans. Now here they are, making one last slow lap of that same pitch, one last hurrah. These men provided unforgettable moments of joy and agony for Everton fans, and as they enter the stadium now the memories come flooding back. Gethin introduces Bob Latchford and Tony Kay. They are hardly recognisable as Latchford the powerful goalscorer and Kay as the tough but creative midfielder. Kay is clearly finding it difficult to walk and so Latchford gives him his arm. They played at different times but today they are teammates.

I am both surprised and delighted to see Tony Kay here. He only played for us for two seasons, but his career was cut short. It wasn't an injury from a bad tackle but a self-inflicted wound. At the age of twenty-four he got caught up in a betting syndicate scandal. It was revealed that he had been bribed to throw a match in 1962 between Ipswich and his team, Sheffield Wednesday, a game that Wednesday lost 2-0. Bizarrely, Kay was voted Man of the Match in the game he was accused of throwing. Two of his teammates, David 'Bronco' Layne and Peter Swan, were also accused. The players also bet on their own side to lose. All three players were convicted of conspiracy to defraud and sentenced to prison with a lifelong ban from football. This all came to light when the *Sunday People* published a story exposing a match-fixing ring within football. By then Kay had been transferred to Everton and was already an England international with a bright future ahead of him. He was twenty-six when he was banned and never kicked another ball in a professional game. Now here he is, over sixty years later, taking in the cheers of the crowd, with some of us remembering what a great footballer he was and what a tragic end to his career it had been.

What could possibly be going through this old man's mind? His punishment was so severe. When a sportsman's career is ended, they are not just losing a job but having their identity stripped away. And Kay's career didn't just end; it was publicly trampled into the dust. Banned from playing for life and then imprisoned for cheating. He had committed a crime, no question, but for a footballer in the Sixties – before the days of huge fees and advertising contracts, when footballers were not yet the hermetically sealed demi-gods who lived on a different planet – it was a life ban and prison.

Why had Kay come at all today? Surely this was a painful reminder for the old man of what his life could have been. Maybe he was here to remind us – and perhaps himself – of who he used to be. His body was no longer strong but perhaps somewhere deep inside him flickered the tenacity and fearlessness he once showed on this very pitch. I hope he heard the crowd shout his name one more time and he got whatever it was he came looking for.

Whoever put his name on today's list of invitees deserves credit. It seems a fairly typical gesture of the club; I've talked to some former Everton players over the years and they all say what a lovely club it was to play for.

Next comes Derek Temple, beloved for his winning goal in the FA Cup Final in 1966. Now eighty-seven years old, he walks slowly in front of the goal at the Stanley Park End and out towards the corner flag. My mind suddenly flashes back to November 1963: I am eight years old, standing behind that same corner flag, watching us play Don Revie's Leeds. There was no love lost between the two teams. Revie had forged a very powerful and physically tough – sometimes verging on violent – group of players. They were probably the most disliked and feared team in the league and that's just how they liked it. They were led by Billy Bremner, a future captain of Scotland who, as P.G. Wodehouse once described another Scotsman, 'could not be confused with a ray of sunshine'. I'm sure our level-headed manager, Harry Catterick, would have told his players in the dressing room before the game that, whatever the provocation, under no circumstances should they retaliate. Walk away; don't let them get to you. Straight after the kick-off, Bremner committed a heavy foul on our centre-forward Fred Pickering. Pickering picked himself up, didn't react and walked away. So far so good. Then, in the fourth minute, Leeds' gifted winger Johnny Giles made a dangerous chest-high tackle on Sandy Brown, our Scottish full-back. Sandy got up and – after a second's consideration, clearly forgetting he wasn't in a pub – punched Giles in full view of the referee, who promptly sent him off. We still had eighty-six minutes to go. At this rate we'd have run out of players by half-time.

I'd like to say the Everton crowd behaved impeccably, but we were incensed and stoked the fetid atmosphere. No one does grievance like us; we've turned it into an art form. The Leeds players and referee alike were booed and abused. Gary Sprake in the Leeds goal was pelted with coins. (Goalkeepers must be grateful that we now live in cashless times.) The atmosphere grew increasingly foul, while the game was turning very nasty. The crowd cheered every flying tackle our players made and loudly booed when one of theirs did the same. I was with my dad, so I didn't feel afraid. To be honest, it was exciting. Such emotion. Such self-righteous anger. And then something happened that shocked the crowd into silence: Willie Bell, the Leeds full-back, smashed into Temple with two feet, catching him on the head and laying him out cold. We thought Temple was dead. Bell wisely stayed down too, and both players were carried off. Nowadays Bell would have been sent off and possibly charged with grievous bodily harm, but he wasn't even cautioned. They were different times.

After that, the atmosphere both on and off the pitch deteriorated even further. In the end the match became unplayable, with missiles peppering the players and the players seeking to kick the opposition instead of the football. The referee, Ken Stokes, took the unprecedented decision of taking both teams off to cool down. Later there was talk that Stokes had considered abandoning the game but had been persuaded by the team captains to carry on. The crowd – having been warned that the game would be over if more missiles were thrown onto the pitch – were slightly calmer and better behaved when the game resumed, and by the final whistle Leeds had clinched a narrow 1-0 victory. After the match, Everton were fined £250 for not controlling their fans, Sandy Brown was suspended for two weeks and that notorious game went down in folklore as The Battle of Goodison. And what of Willie Bell who nearly ended Temple's career? He popped back onto the pitch and scored the winner. Don't you love football?

I wonder now as I watch 87-year-old Temple walk slowly over the spot where he was laid out cold all those years ago if he too had a similar flashback. Did a frisson shoot through his old bones as he recalled that terrible moment just before he passed out?

I'm jolted from my reverie by the irrepressible Gethin telling the crowd that we've got a lot to get through and that he can't do it all on his own. So is this the moment Paul McCartney comes out? No, not yet. Instead, Gethin introduces the man who is not only an avid Evertonian and regular at Goodison Park but who also won the WBC Cruiserweight title in May 2016 here on this very pitch: none other than Tony 'Bomber' Bellew. He still looks good; Stephen Graham would probably play him in the movie. He gets a huge welcome from the crowd, who are now marinated in a warm bath of memories and togetherness.

As the heroes of our all-conquering 1980s team wander onto the pitch, in the centre circle Gethin interviews two of the mainstays of that group: captain Peter Reid and Andy Gray, our centre-forward who scored some crucial goals on big occasions. Both are good talkers. Reid is emotional and pays tribute to a club he clearly loves. He generally uses swearing as punctuation but, on this occasion, he reins it in and manages to avoid dropping the F-bomb. He tells the crowd that, while it's sad to be leaving 'the grand old lady, they are the grand old people.' The crowd goes wild. Given what he could have said, most parents with children in the ground are relieved.

Next Gray takes the microphone. A professional pundit and after-dinner speaker these days, he talks fluently about his time at Everton and especially that magical night when we came from behind to batter Bayern Munich 3-1 in the semis of the European Cup Winners' Cup in 1985, often regarded as the greatest night at Goodison Park. Looking emotional now, he finishes off with a catch in his voice: 'Today we may be leaving Goodison, but Goodison will never leave us.' The crowd roars again. I don't think Gray even got that sort of response after scoring against Bayern.

As if that's not enough, we're now invited to watch the stage in front of Gwladys Street, the home end, where I stood with my dad in the Sixties and Seventies. Tony Bellew is there with two of the most iconic figures in Everton's history: one a Scot who literally shed blood for the team; the other a local lad who exploded onto the scene as a sixteen-year-old but then had to move away to play at the level his talent demanded. 'Please welcome Duncan Ferguson and Wayne Rooney.' There is more rapturous cheering and chanting; we might die of a nostalgia overdose. The two ex-players clamber up onto the stage, and the sight is not without its visual comedy: Ferguson is six foot three; Rooney most definitely isn't.

Ferguson, who could never be described as reserved, can't contain his feelings and no matter what question is put to him by Bellew, just holds his arms aloft like he did when he'd scored, and screams 'Up the Toffees'. But don't be fooled by his natural ebullience; he also possesses a sharp wit. Asked the previous day in a radio interview what his favourite goal was for Everton, he replied it was the diving header against Manchester United in 2005 that secured our Champions League qualifying spot, before adding drily: 'For our younger listeners, Manchester United used to be a good football team.'

Rooney then talks about his love for the club. He was one of those local lads who achieve the dream of most young football-loving boys: he played for the team he supported *and* scored on his debut. His speech today is generous, paying tribute today to the fans and referring to the 'ups and downs' they've had. A number of fans vilified him when he left the club – idiots with abandonment issues who refused to see that it wasn't Rooney at fault but Everton for not being good enough to keep him. He had cost us nothing, given us two seasons of magic and then a transfer fee of £30 million in 2004, yet still some halfwits complained. They felt betrayed and made their feelings known, rendering what must have been a difficult decision for the eighteen-year-old Rooney even more painful. But he was no fool; he wasn't going to make the same mistake as Steven Gerrard on the other side of Stanley Park and not meet his potential by allowing sentimentality to overcome common sense and healthy ambition.

Rooney came back towards the end of his career and gave us forty more games and some flashes of genius. The goal he scored from just inside his own half against West Ham, which completed a hat-trick, is regarded as one of the best ever seen at Goodison. And here he is today with a big grin stretched across his now ample chops, lapping up the crowd's chanting of his name. It's a moving sight. No hard feelings, Wayne. This day just keeps getting better and better. Still no Paul McCartney, though.

Now it's the turn of the current team to do their 'lap of honour', in what is perhaps the only mistake in the day's order of events. It must be hard for the current underachieving squad to follow dozens of former play-ers who won trophies and took the club to the top of the league and several cup finals. It might have been better to do this at the beginning and then bring on the legends. But on they came, holding babies, surrounded by toddlers, accompanied by wives and girlfriends decked in designer outfits, drifting across the turf. I wondered how many of them really wanted to be there. Did I detect a certain reluctance, even sheepishness from a few of them? Some hadn't been at the club that long and others were likely to be offloaded now the new owners were in charge. I can't help but feel this part of the celebrations takes the air out of the occasion a little. I want to spend more time with the legends of the past.

Fortunately our host Gethin, who is doing a great job corralling players for on-pitch interviews, manages to elevate the moment by grabbing one of the current squad favourites, Seamus Coleman, already a club legend. Coleman must be our best-value signing ever, coming from Sligo Rovers in 2009 for £60,000. His commitment to the club has put to shame more expensive and flashier signings during his time. He is an articulate and serious Irishman, and I can see him returning to Everton as a manager at some point in the future.

Our current manager, David Moyes, now takes to the pitch and the tireless Gethin peppers him with questions. Moyes is not given to sentimental musings about past glories. He pays tribute to the crowd and then turns to the directors' box and says, 'I hope the new owners can recognise what they're seeing here today. Because this is to be built up, rebuilt, brought back, get us back to where we all belong.' It's a Braveheart moment from our Scottish leader and he gets the crowd to roar its approval.

I'm pleased that Moyes is taking us into the new stadium. When he was reappointed I was neither overwhelmed nor underwhelmed, I was just sort of 'whelmed'. Like many others, I thought he was a sensible bet but not that exciting. To give him credit, though, he took a dangerously hapless squad who seemed to be circling the plughole for the third season in a row and strung together a run of eight games unbeaten. Within a couple of months we were clear of the drop zone and found ourselves in the unfamiliar uplands of mid-table mediocrity. Perhaps Moyes will defy the old rule of 'never go back'.

There is a heartwarming interview now on the stage at the other end of the pitch. Some players from the women's squad are telling us just how excited they are to be taking possession of the 'Old Lady of Goodison'. The crowd cheers and applauds. The Old Lady will live on courtesy of the young women; again, the club gets it right. Could this be a new Everton FC taking shape – a club that makes smart decisions?

The speeches and interviews are over and now we're told we are in for a musical treat on the centre stage. This must be Paul McCartney, surely? 'Please welcome Bill Ryder-Jones and his band.' Bill is a local musician who was in a band called The Coral. He is good and gets the crowd singing with a lively version of one of our anthems, 'Spirit of The Blues', and then a member of his band sporting a cloth cap like he's in *Peaky Blinders* plays 'Theme from Z Cars' on a French horn, which is brave. It's a slow rendition, and his cheeks bulge with the effort of squeezing out each drawling note. He can't possibly take the tune at its normal tempo or he'd have a respiratory collapse.

We are now nearly an hour in and presumably somewhere towards the end. Despite some very moving moments, I've managed to keep my composure. But just when I think it's safe, Ryder-Jones begins to sing 'In My Life' by John Lennon: 'There are places I remember...' And that's it, I'm gone. The tears start to flow, the shoulders start to heave, and I'm sobbing. It is my favourite Beatles song. When I appeared on *Desert Island Discs* in 2010 it was the record I wanted to keep when Kirsty Young asked me which of the eight discs I would save. The song kills me, it always has, but today it slaughters me.

'I know I'll often stop and think about them.'

I think of my dad, who first brought me here. Today is his birthday; he would have been ninety-five. How he would have loved to have sat with his brother and the three grandsons he never got to meet.

I think of my quietly spoken stepfather, John, who sat next to me from 1995 until his death. He would hand out those famous Everton toffees that give us our nickname.

I think of my cousin Gerard, who died too young in 2020. He would have been here standing in between his father, my uncle Gerard, and his big sister, Sharon.

I think of my younger self coming here religiously to home games and the reserve games in the 1960s and 70s, and then – to my shame – how I didn't come for many years as I moved away and tried to reinvent myself. I think of how I began the journey to come home thirty years ago after a chance conversation with Bill Kenwright.

I think of Bill and how much he loved Everton and what a bitter end he had, carrying the can for the hopeless Farad Moshiri.

I'm crying for all of them and I'm grateful to them all too. So many memories and all because we loved the same football team.

I feel an arm around me. 'Are you OK, Dad?' It's my son George. By the time he's my age, he and his brothers will have more memories of the new stadium than of Goodison.

In the end Paul McCartney didn't show up, but who cares? John Lennon did. The final moments of this quite magnificent send-off to Goodison unfold and – just in case there's anyone not in tears – the cool dude in the cloth cap whips out his French horn one more time and does another round of the 'Theme from Z Cars' played as a sort of 'Last Post' as the Everton flag is lowered. And that's it: everyone is dabbing their eyes or openly crying; some are sobbing into their neighbour's shoulder.

If anyone looking at this extraordinary, intimate moment shared by 40,000 people still thinks supporting your football team is just a pastime, then they need to seek help. It has been a classy ending to a beautifully staged day.

Goodbye, Goodison. I'll always remember the good times and, try as I might, I can't forget the bad.

2

Catching Evertonitis

I CAN'T remember the moment I decided I was going to be an Everton fan. There is no memory of an elective choice; I grew up just knowing in my bones that I was one. But how did this happen?

Well, my father was not an entirely rational man. My uncle told me recently that, during the Korean War, when my father was stationed in Japan for two years with the Royal Navy only ten weeks after he and my mother were married, he would send her money every week to help her save for a house. My father told her that he didn't mind where he lived as long as it was within a mile of Goodison Park.

As soon as I was toilet-trained he took me to my first Everton game at Goodison. That day in 1959 we walked the half-mile up Walton Lane to the ground. On our left was Anfield cemetery – the 'dead centre' of Liverpool, as we locals cheerfully called it – and then on past Gwladys St Primary school, which was soon to become my first place of learning, before entering the stadium. My father spent the match smoking his John Player unfiltered ciggies and screaming instructions to the players and abuse at the referee while I stood on the seat and tried to throw Jelly Babies at the players, much to the annoyance of the man sitting two rows down on whose head I was bouncing the sweets. I have no memory of this event. Like every adult, I have stories of my childhood in which I play a prominent role but of which I have no memory. The memories are implanted by the unreliable accounts of our parents. (There are also stories in which I play a lead role when I was a grown man in the 1980s and of which I have no memory, but that's for entirely different reasons.)

My father's strategy in taking me to see his beloved Everton at such a young age was, he explained, that my merely being at the game would initiate the process of turning me into a Blue; that even in my almost pre-cognitive state, by some osmotic process, being among other devoted Everton fans meant I too would become an Evertonian. I would, he hoped, catch 'Evertonitis'. He was clearly not taking any chances with the footballing soul of his only son. You see, half a mile away, across Stanley Park, a rival football team was growing in stature. They were called Liverpool and there was no way any son of his would wear a red football shirt.

The fear of every parent who is a lifelong supporter of a football team is that their child will choose a different team and break their heart. And that is why many years later, in 2007, the night before every Everton Saturday home game, I would drive with my three-year-old son Jack two hundred miles from my home in London to that same house from which I set foot in 1959 to see my first game. Jack and I would stay the night with my mum, who still lived in the same house, and we would walk the same route as my father and I did and then take our places in the same stand as my father and I did nearly fifty years before. My wife, Karen, like my mother before her, not unreasonably asked what possible purpose it would serve taking a child who could barely walk and speak to sit through a ninety-minute game, none of which he would understand. She added: 'He will probably fall asleep after half an hour. He'll be bored.' I hate it when people meet my unrealistic goals with common sense. She was right, of course: at every game in those early years, Jack would eat the entire bag of sweets his adoring Nana June had given him and then slip into a sugar-coma just before half-time. But I persisted; like my father, I was taking no chances. Also like my father, I lived near a football club – a much more successful club than Everton, called Chelsea. No one in their right mind wants their child to become a Chelsea fan (apart from Chelsea fans, of course, who are, by definition, not in their right mind). I couldn't put my little boy at that kind of risk. I loved him too much.

Back in the 1960s I only attended a game when my father wasn't working on a Saturday. It was always a treat when we went to the game; I loved spending time with my dad. He was great company: funny, the teller of great stories – some of which were probably not in The Good Parents' Handbook – and he was smart. He was highly intelligent but, like a lot of men of his generation in Liverpool, he left school at fourteen. Apparently he won a scholarship to St Edward's, a very good grammar school, but his father told him he couldn't go. He was one of nine children living in a two-bedroom house in Old Swan and he needed to contribute, so my fourteen-year-old dad got a job. Aged sixteen he joined the Royal Navy. He told me the main reason for enlisting was a desire for his own bed.

As soon as I was old enough, my dad stopped forking out for seats in the stands on the grounds that, not only was it more expensive, but the atmosphere wasn't as good as standing on the terraces. My dad would stand on the terraces but he would place me in a specially cordoned-off segment of the ground reserved for fans under the age of sixteen. It was felt this was a safer space for young boys. In those days the attendance at Goodison could sometimes be over fifty thousand, and in moments of high drama the crowd would sway – at times dangerously so. So it was considered to be safer to place one's child inside a smaller enclosure that would be protected from the ebbs and flows of a massive crowd.

This sanctuary was called the Boys' Pen. The dictionary definition of 'pen' is 'a small enclosure in which sheep, pigs or other farm animals are kept', which is a fairly accurate description of what the two hours spent cooped up in the Boys' Pen felt like. It was a wedge-shaped space in the south-east corner of the ground, crammed with scores of boys aged from eight to around fifteen, where a fortnightly live experiment in Darwinian evolutionary theory was conducted. Social anthropologists could have written academic papers about what went on in that hellhole on a Saturday afternoon. One thing it wasn't was a safe space. Before one game a slightly larger boy appeared from nowhere and headbutted me. As I picked myself off the floor, nursing my bloody nose and pretending like it was nothing really, the headbutter took a long look at me, smiled apologetically, and said: 'Sorry mate, I thought you were someone else.'

3

The Best Team
in the Land

MY FATHER worked shifts as a boiler operator at
Clarence Dock power station so was regularly unavail-
able to take me to the game and there was no way my
mother would allow me to go on my own. My mum
was an anxious woman and saw danger in most situ-
ations. 'Be careful' was her motto. Even a short trip
to Walton Hall Park for a kickabout was treated like
I was off to the Front. So, on the days my dad worked
and I was prevented from enjoying the *Lord of the Flies*
re-enactment in the Pen, I was stuck at home. On these
Saturdays I had to *listen* to the game. Not on the radio
but out in the street. My house was only half a mile
away from Goodison so during the match I could stand

outside our house and try to deduce exactly what was going on inside the stadium by listening to the various reactions of the crowd.

Fifty thousand people witnessing a near-miss had a distinctive sound to it. A brief roar followed by applause was a brave tackle by an Everton player that left the opposing player writhing on the floor in agony. The huge and prolonged cheer accompanying a goal was easy to spot, of course, but loud booing was open to interpretation. Like a sommelier washing a glass of Claret around his mouth, I would savour the sound for a few seconds, weighing up the options. Could that have been a bad foul by Billy Bremner on one of our players? Or was it just some terrible refereeing decision against one of us?

The one thing I had to admit was that our crowd didn't have the musical repertoire of the Liverpool fans. It was the mid-1960s and The Beatles were dominating the charts, but it was the Kop not the Gwladys Street end who gave full voice to their hits. The gift that was the proximity of Goodison Park was offset by the curse that Anfield was also within earshot of my street on their matchdays. Whenever Liverpool were at home, I had to endure the quite magnificent choral singing of

'She Loves You' by the Kopites. It really annoyed me; they had hijacked my favourite band.

My other activity on Everton matchdays when Dad was working was altogether more lucrative and saw an early blossoming of my entrepreneurial – some might say criminal – instincts. My street was a quiet cul-de-sac with hardly any cars in it. My family didn't have a car in those days, and neither did most of our neighbours. As we were only ten minutes' walk away from Goodison, our road was the perfect place for those fans who needed to park their cars. My mates and I saw a gap in the market. From about 1.30 p.m. we would loiter aimlessly in the street, maybe kicking a ball and looking for all the world like a bunch of innocent nine-year-olds. A Hillman Imp, Vauxhall Victor, Ford Cortina, Corsair or even an Austin 1100 – the kind of cars that roamed the highways and byways of Britain in those days – would innocently pull into our street and start to park. At this point, the movie soundtrack of this scene would introduce a *Jaws*-like threatening theme as, like a school of piranha sensing some unwitting prey, we would drop the pretence of playing football and instead swarm around the driver: 'Can we mind your car for you, please sir?' To be fair, most punters knew the score. They'd toss us a shilling and we'd promise to 'look after' their vehicle. We understood one another. Job done. However, every now and again someone who was new to the street and new to our line of business might question the value of our commodity. Perhaps they'd say: 'Why would my car need minding?' We'd smile warmly at the naivety of the question and quietly point out that there were some unsavoury types knocking about, some as young as us, who would maybe let the tyres down or scratch the paintwork, so wasn't a shilling or two worth it to insure against any such occurrence? It would be a shame, would it not, for anything to happen to such a nice car, sir? There would be a pause as the message was received. The driver would assess the situation and a shilling would be forthcoming. 'Nice doing business with you, sir.' Looking after about twenty cars on a Saturday wasn't enough to retire on but it did keep us in a steady supply of Bazooka Joes, Flying Saucers and Fruit Salads for the whole weekend.

In the 1962/63 season Everton were doing well. We had a strong team and sat top of the league, although Spurs were breathing down our necks and they had Jimmy Greaves, the First Division's leading scorer with 37 goals. On 11 May, the last day of the season, we were at home to Fulham, who were sitting in sixteenth place. If we could beat Fulham, the trophy would be ours. It was a game I couldn't miss. The problem was my dad was working that Saturday and he was very conscientious about his work. There'd be no bunking off for him, no matter how hard I tried to persuade him. My mum was also at work on a Saturday. She was a waitress in George Henry Lee, a department store owned by John Lewis that had a posh restaurant on the top floor with white tablecloths and open sandwiches. The only other adult in the house was my maternal grandfather, who had descended on us after my grandmother was killed in a car accident, and he was never going to offer to take me (for reasons that will soon become clear).

So there I was, standing in the street, trying to decipher what was going on inside the stadium during the most momentous Everton game of my life. I heard cheers – some short, a few loud and long (goals, surely?) – and of course lots of outraged booing. It sounded like we were winning. But how to be sure? There was only one way: I was going to try and get into Goodison to catch the last twenty minutes. I knew if my mother found out I'd be in trouble, but I've always thought it's better to ask for forgiveness than for permission. (I just wish I hadn't shared that advice with my teenage sons many years later.)

I ran up Walton Lane, pumped with adrenalin, thrilled that I was going to witness the greatest achievement for any English football club and thrilled that I was doing something so incredibly naughty. I was soon on Goodison Road, standing by the side entrance to the Gwladys Street end. The seconds were ticking away, and the noise of the crowd was telling me this was a match you had to see. It was a warm, sunny day, I was eight years of age, and I had never been this excited.

At three-quarters time, with a good twenty minutes left on the clock, the doors to the ground were flung open to let out anyone who wished to leave early and beat the crowds, but no one was leaving today. I darted in and burrowed deep into the crowd behind the goal. I didn't feel scared in the slightest: large football crowds in those days – despite the density of the bodies standing sardined together on sloping terraces – showed remarkable delicacy in protecting a child in danger of being crushed or an adult feeling faint. At those moments it was as if the crowd was one large, intelligent organism, and the frightened child or breathless adult would be passed seamlessly down a moving hill of hands and deposited safely by the pitch, where they could sit out the game in safety.

I found a place just to the left of the goal that Everton were attacking – and there were my heroes in the flesh, only a few yards away. And *yes!* we were winning 3-1 by half-time. Our Welsh striker, Roy Vernon, had scored two and our Scottish winger – Alex Scott, signed only two months earlier from Rangers for £36,000* – had nabbed one. We were all over them. In the crowd without my dad for the first time, I felt very grown up but I wished he was there to see this. We were battering Fulham, and they were no pushover. They had some great players in that team – full-back George Cohen (who would play in the 1966 World Cup-winning team), England inside-forward Johnny Haynes, international midfielder Alan Mullery (a hardman with the distinction of being the first player to be sent off in an England game), and

---

* Scott's nickname was Chico, which I think he was given because he had dark wavy hair and could have passed for Spanish. In those days you were a foreign player if you came from outside Liverpool.

future England manager Bobby Robson – but today they were no match for the mighty Blues.*

A party atmosphere was building in Goodison as we drew nearer to the final whistle then, with seven minutes to go, the ball went wide to Scott, who went haring down the right wing with his distinctive stooping run and crossed it into the Fulham area…

It's at this point, dear reader, that my memory fails me in recalling exactly what happened next. I know what I *thought* I saw, but now I'm not sure. Did my view get impeded by a crowd surge? Or was I distracted, trying to keep my balance in the heaving mass of much bigger human beings jammed in behind the goal? I want to say Roy Vernon met the cross with his head and it flew into the net, completing his hat-trick. But did he meet it with his head? Maybe he took a touch and passed it into the net with his left foot? Or was it his right? I've tried to find the highlights of the game on YouTube but there aren't any. We take for the

---

* My hero, Alex Young, our centre forward, didn't get on the score sheet that day but he was my favourite. My school was next door to the stadium, and one day I saw him walking down the street in a suit. He looked strange; I expected him to be always wearing his blue and white kit even when he went to the shops.

granted the ease with which we can access footage to pretty much any game these days. Nowadays I'm willing to believe my memory is a liar because it's been proved to be so by science. In his brilliant podcast series, *Revisionist History*, Malcolm Gladwell reveals that after 9/11 neuroscientists in America asked a large group of people who had escaped the Twin Towers, or had been close by and had witnessed their collapse, to recount their memories of that unforgettable experience. Every year they would be asked to do the same: write down exactly where they were and what they saw. After twelve years, sixty per cent of them had changed their story to a significant degree. And that is an event that scientists call a 'flashbulb memory', created when an event is so vivid it imprints itself on the memory. So forgive me if I can't say without any doubt whether Vernon scored with his head, his left foot, right foot or with another part of his anatomy. The important thing, though, is that he did score, and the crowd went nuts – and me with it.

The final whistle blew, and the score from White Hart Lane came in: Spurs had been beaten 0-1 by Manchester City, who nevertheless were relegated on the same day. The teams went off and within minutes the Everton players were in the directors' box up in the stands, being presented with the First Division trophy. Vernon, who was the club captain as well as the three-goal hero, held the cup above his head.

We always knew we were the best team in the city, and now we were crowned the best team in the land. Surely we were on the brink of a sustained period of dominance. What could possibly go wrong?

4
Shankly

LIVERPOOL FC, that's what went wrong. The season after our great league victory in 1963, Liverpool went and won the league in 1964, and the following year they won the FA Cup. Something was happening across Stanley Park, and it didn't bode well for us.

Within three years of being promoted to the First Division, Liverpool had won two major trophies under the auspices of their charismatic Scottish manager, Bill Shankly. Under him Liverpool FC would be reinvented. He created an ethos – a blueprint for continued success – that continued long after he left the club. He made the players, and the fans, believe they were special, and turned the club into a powerful brand. He said of Anfield: 'This is my church,' and talked of

Liverpool supporters worshipping there: 'I think it's more than fanaticism. It's a religion'. As if to emphasise his religious zeal, he signed a striker called St John.

Teams would fear going to Anfield as Liverpool embarked on a decades-long spree of winning trophies in England and Europe. They became one of the most famous clubs in world football, and it all started with the genius of Bill Shankly.

I hated Bill Shankly.

5

1966 and the Centre of the Universe

1966 was a big year for football. In the city of Liverpool and across the country there was great euphoria. Nowhere was that felt more than in our two-bedroom house in Wellbrow Road, Walton, Liverpool 4, where I had lived with my mother and father, June and Jimmy, from a few days after my birth in 1955. It was just the three of us, and I'm told we were very happy for the first four years of my life. Then in 1959 tragedy struck.

My maternal grandmother – or Nana, as she preferred to be called – was coming home one night after working late in The Crocodile, a fashionable restaurant that she managed in the city centre. According to family folklore, she had changed her night off from 3 November to

5 November so she could spend Guy Fawkes Night with her only grandchild. Uncharacteristically, she accepted a lift from the taxi-driver husband of one of the young women who worked for her. She had no reason to believe he was over the limit; in those days, drink-driving was commonplace. Driving up Everton Valley, the taxi shot a red light just as a Liverpool Corporation bus was coming across the road. In the ensuing collision, the taxi driver and my grandmother were killed. She was forty-nine.

The shockwaves devastated the family – particularly my mum, who had worked with her mother since leaving school at the age of fourteen, and completely worshipped her. And now her mum, her heroine, was gone. One of my first memories is of my mother hearing the news that November night, screaming and running around the room as if she was on fire. She would spend the next thirty years trying to put that fire out with alcohol until miraculously she got sober in 1990.

One of the other consequences of that night was the addition of my grandfather, Tommy, to our household. Although only in his early fifties, he decided he needed looking after and promptly turned up on our doorstep with his suitcase, asking my mother to do just that. Whether out of pity or still in shock, she agreed –

much against my father's will. We had been three and now we were four. I was to be moved to the tiny room at the back of the house – the box room – and our new resident would go into the middle room.

Now, I want to be as generous as I can to my long-departed grandfather, Tommy Fee. After all, he had just lost his wife in tragic circumstances and was no doubt in dreadful shock at the sudden loss. He would grieve and weep over this loss whenever he had too much to drink, which was often, but in truth he had not treated this now much-missed wife well while she was alive. My grandmother had been the main bread-winner, had spoiled her husband with fancy clothes and a car when no one else in the street had a car, and he had repaid her by doing exactly as he pleased. We want to like the people who are suffering a tragic loss, and I can now see my grandfather must have felt abandoned and lonely after Nana died, but Tommy Fee was living proof that you can be both a victim of terrible misfortune and a bit of an arsehole. Unlike my father, he wasn't an intellectually bright man and he never said anything remotely funny. He wasn't generous, and he wasn't that interested in his grandson or indeed anyone except himself. Yet these were minor defects compared to his main fault, which my dad and I couldn't forgive: Tommy was a Liverpool fan. Not that he ever went to a game, but that didn't stop him crowing about how great 'his' team were doing.

Being an Evertonian in the same house as a Liverpool fan – even one as lapsed as my grandfather – was not much fun. Liverpool had made sure of the First Division trophy after a 2-0 win at Anfield against Chelsea on 30 April 1966. It was their second league triumph in only three seasons. It was tough going some nights in our house when Tommy, seated in the chair near the coal fire, would read the glowing reports from the sports pages of the *Liverpool Echo* about how marvellous Roger Hunt was or what a great captain Tommy Smith had been that season or what a genius their manager Bill Shankly was. I could feel the tension rise when Tommy, brandishing the evening *Echo*, would say: 'Did you read this about what Shankly has said?' My father and I would show no interest at all, but that wouldn't deter him and we would have to listen to another deathless quote. He wasn't really talking to us, though, he was just enjoying one his favourite pastimes: listening to the sound of his own voice.

• • •

Around the same time that Liverpool had secured the league title, Everton had quietly put together a successful run in the FA Cup. After beating Manchester City in the sixth round and then Manchester United in the semi-final, we were to face Sheffield Wednesday in the final on 14 May 1966. In the two weeks leading up to the final there was great excitement in my house – for my dad and me, at least. I hoped we could go down to Wembley, but tickets were scarce. The official allocation had long gone and now they were only accessible through touts. There were rumours circulating of the odd ticket being sold in The Hermitage – our local – but nothing came of it. Then suddenly one ticket became available. The price was £7, or around £100 today. My father plucked up courage and decided to consult my mother as to the viability of such a purchase. My mother was the Chancellor of the Exchequer of Wellbrow Road. She ran the household and its finances; nothing was bought or sold without her sign-off. Her seemingly bottomless handbag, from which I think celestial light and heavenly music emanated when she opened it, was the seat of power in our family home.

But my father was no slouch in presenting a good case. He had honed his negotiating skills over the years with a strange weekly ritual performed each Wednesday evening. He was paid in cash weekly, on Thursdays, and by Wednesday he would have run out of money. This meant that, in order to finance an evening in the pub, he would have to approach my mother and try to prise a fiver out of the legendary handbag. This single-act play was re-enacted every week for an audience of one – me, quietly having my tea and toast before I was ordered to bed.

So, with the Cup Final only days away, my father was now faced with a much bigger test of his negotiation skills: the £7 FA Cup Final ticket. History doesn't give us the details of the conversation between my mother and father; unlike Alexander Hamilton, I wasn't 'in the room where it happened'. But suffice to say, the purchase was approved: the family had a ticket. Now, you're thinking that obviously *I* wouldn't be going to Wembley on my own, being an eleven-year-old. No, surely my dad – a lifelong Everton fan who religiously stood in the Paddock at Goodison Park, often with one of his five brothers – would be the Charlie Bucket of this story. You would think that if there were any justice in the world, he would get the golden ticket, right? Wrong. Here's the surprising twist.

My mother had a younger brother, Tommy Fee Jnr, who had recently returned to Liverpool from New Zealand after a seven-year absence. Apparently, when he was nineteen he joined the merchant navy and found himself bound for New Zealand. There, obviously liking what he saw, he jumped ship and went on the run as an illegal alien. When the authorities finally tracked him down, they discovered that he had married a Māori princess and had a child with her and so he couldn't be deported because he was now by marriage a member of the Māori aristocracy. Back in Liverpool, the family was distraught, not knowing where or how he was. His doting mother, my grandmother, would never see him again. Even after her death in the car accident in 1959, Tommy Fee Jnr didn't come home and consequently his father never forgave him for what he saw as a terrible betrayal. But seven years later, in early 1966, news arrived that he was coming home. And where was he going to live? Wellbrow Road, of course, and the four of us became five.

And by some twisted family logic – he hadn't seen Everton for such a long time, wouldn't it be a nice treat for him to go to Wembley to see the team in a final? – the £7 FA Cup Final ticket was the fatted calf for the prodigal son who had finally come home. The thing about Tommy Jnr is that (unlike Tommy Fee Snr) everyone liked him, and so he was sent off to Wembley with our best wishes as a representative of the family. One of our own was going to see the Blues win the Cup.

When the big day arrived, I was selfishly thrilled that my dad and I would be watching the game together on our black and white television (colour TV still being a year away). The fly in the ointment was the presence of my grandfather the Liverpool fan, whom I was increasingly resenting, and who often couldn't keep his mouth shut when he came home after a few beers in the pub on a Saturday afternoon. And when Tommy Fee Snr came back from the pub at 2.45 p.m. that Saturday he had definitely had a few beers. My father and his two mates had also been to the pub and brought back a couple of crates of ale in anticipation of a great Everton victory and the ensuing celebrations. I hadn't been to the pub, being only eleven, but was allowed to take a sip of my dad's drink.

We all assumed our positions in front of the telly (me entirely kitted out in blue and white: a blue tracksuit, blue and white scarf and a strange plastic blue and white boater) and watched the pre-match entertainment, the military band playing 'Abide with Me', and the teams coming out onto the pitch.

Everton were led by Harry Catterick, who had already delivered a league championship trophy in 1963. I was glued to the television as Jack Taylor, the referee who would go on to officiate the 1974 World Cup Final, blew the whistle to start the game. But with just four minutes of the game gone, disaster struck: Jim McCalliog, Sheffield Wednesday's young Scottish striker, smashed the ball past Gordon West to make it 1-0. To say my father, his two Evertonian friends and I were stunned doesn't quite cover it. Every football fan will know how it feels when your team goes a goal down, especially in an important game like a cup final. It's an overwhelming combination of denial, shock, dread and despair. We were speechless. Fortunately, there was someone close by who could step in, break the awkward silence and give us all the benefit of his deep football knowledge: yes, my grandfather. Five pints of bitter had bestowed upon him the gift of insightful analysis of what we had just witnessed.

'They're a very good side, this Sheffield Wednesday team,' he opined, before warming to his role: 'That was a good goal. They'll take some beating.'

I could see in my father's expression that a beating was what he'd like to give his father-in-law at that precise moment.

The first half ended with us still trailing 1-0, and the interval was miserable. We didn't need Jimmy Hill and Kenneth Wolstenholme to assess the first half, we had our own pundit in an armchair right in front of us. Impervious to the death stares he was drawing from his audience, my grandfather went on and on, extolling the virtues of 'this talented, young Sheffield Wednesday team'. The ability to read the room was not one of his qualities. Thankfully the second half commenced, and my dad requested quiet concentration on the match. My grandfather shut up and sipped his beer. The beer in the Evertonian crates remained untouched – there was nothing to celebrate so far. And matters were about to get a lot worse.

In the fifty-seventh minute Sheffield Wednesday went further ahead when David Ford clipped one neatly past West. We were shattered. At two goals down, with only thirty minutes left, no one would have put money on us lifting the cup. I took my blue and white striped plastic boater off; you can only wear something as ludicrous as that when you're winning.

My grandfather, perhaps sensing he was now at something akin to a funeral, decided to adopt a slightly more conciliatory tone: 'There's no shame in being beaten by this Sheffield team.'

'For fuck's sake, Tommy, give it a rest,' one of my dad's mates suggested.

'I'm only saying…'

'Shut up, Tommy, for fuck's sake,' my dad shouted.

The gloves were off. Four Evertonians – wound up and looking down the barrel of a humiliating defeat, with Liverpool already crowned as champions – were on the edge. The tension in the room was almost tangible, like that in the scene in *Goodfellas* where Joe Pesci suddenly shoots the waiter. I had visions of my mother coming home from work to find my dad and his mates burying my grandfather's corpse in the backyard. But then two minutes later something extraordinary happened: Mike Trebilcock – Everton's first Black player, recently signed from lower-league Plymouth Argyle and a surprise choice for the Cup Final ahead of Everton favourite Fred Pickering – popped up and stuck one past England goalkeeper, Ron Springett.

Five minutes later we were cheering and hugging: Trebilcock had scored an equaliser. Having spent most of the season out with an injury, he was something of an unknown quantity to the Everton fans, but now he was immediately promoted to 'legend' status. The jubilation in my house was marked by the cracking open of the first few beer bottles stacked against the wall. Were we about to witness a footballing miracle?

At Wembley the Evertonian half of the crowd went nuts too. In fact, one fan was so transported by the equaliser that he ran onto the pitch to congratulate Trebilcock. This fan was not built to run a marathon and would nowadays be the 'before' picture in an Ozempic ad, but he could move over the short distance and so a young uniformed copper, helmet bobbing on his head, was finding it hard to catch him. The policeman made a desperate lunge and managed to grab the man's jacket (yes, he was smartly dressed as no one wore club colours back then) but the fan elegantly shimmied and slipped out of the coat, leaving the young constable falling on his face and clutching a crumpled piece of tweed. The crowd roared in delight. Which football fan, especially those from Liverpool, doesn't like to see a 'bizzy' make a bit of a tit of himself? Greatly encouraged by this escape from police custody and by the crowd's cheering, the fan was making his way towards Gordon West, our goalkeeper, apparently planning to ask him not to let in any more goals. But before he could deliver his coaching advice, he was jumped by another officer and then several others and was led away. That fan's name was Eddie Cavanagh. He started the game as an anonymous Evertonian, one of thousands, and ended it with his place firmly secured in Everton folklore. It was said he didn't have to buy a drink in a Liverpool pub for the rest of his life.

With twenty minutes to go, it was still anybody's game. Everton's equaliser had heartened my dad and I, and we were now shouting tactics at the telly: 'Play it wide!' 'Shoot!' 'Get rid!' My grandfather, on the other hand, was a quieter figure in the armchair, perhaps baffled that this 'very good Sheffield side' wasn't delivering on his promise. Maybe he was silently praying to the football gods for a late Wednesday winner. If so, his prayers went unanswered: with fifteen minutes to go, the ball was booted upfield and an exhausted Gerry Young, the Sheffield Wednesday defender, tried to trap it in the centre circle but it slipped under his foot. It was pounced on by our winger Derek Temple, who charged down the pitch with Ron Springett coming at him with arms wide. I've seen these chances missed hundreds of times. We held our breath for what seemed like hours, but Temple coolly met his destiny and clipped the ball past the goalkeeper and into the net. Cue mayhem at Wembley and mayhem at Wellbrow Road. We cheered, we punched the air in a 'we proved you wrong' gesture, and one of my dad's mates ruffled my grandfather's hair and hugged him perhaps a little too tightly. We were in heaven. I had rarely seen my dad so deliriously happy, and it was a lovely feeling to see him unbridled in his joy.

The last fifteen minutes were tense – the fans feeling like we were kicking every ball – but there were moments of individual heroism. Our right half-back Jimmy Gabriel, his socks characteristically round his ankles, kept the ball by the corner flag for an age and was cheered by the fans for his efforts. And then it was all over. We had done it: one of the greatest comebacks in FA Cup Final history.

Princess Margaret presented our captain, Brian Labone, with the cup, which he held aloft to a full Wembley stadium. As was the custom in those days, both sets of fans had stayed to applaud the teams and to congratulate the winners. Both sets of fans were savouring their day out at Wembley, knowing they might not be back for some time.

Later that summer, Wembley would host another famous final, when England beat West Germany and so filled English hearts with national pride and set unrealistic expectations of every England men's team for the following (as I write) fifty-nine years. Next year Baddiel and Skinner will have to update that bloody song from thirty years to sixty years of hurt.

For Everton fans the post-World Cup euphoria was extended when it was announced that Alan Ball, one of the breakout stars of the winning England team, was signing for us for a British-record fee of £110,000. Just days before he signed, I went to Goodison to see the Charity Shield match (now the Community Shield) played between the First Division champions and the FA Cup winners. That year it meant we were kicking off the season with a Merseyside derby.

It was a hot August day. Dad and I were situated just to the left of the Gwladys Street goal. Out onto the pitch ran Roger Hunt, Liverpool's inside-forward, and Ray Wilson, our left-back. Hunt was clutching the league trophy, Wilson held the FA Cup, and between them they were holding aloft the Jules Rimet trophy, the World Cup. I've never been so proud. It was a perfect moment: I was standing in the heart of Goodison, my spiritual home, watching two World Cup winners – one a Red, one a Blue – who had also won the two major domestic trophies that year. The Beatles were number one with the double A side of 'Yellow Submarine' and 'Eleanor Rigby'. The sun was shining. The crowds were singing. Liverpool was the centre of the universe. What could possibly go wrong?

Liverpool won 1-0, that's what went wrong. I can still hear the ball's swishing sound as it slid down the back of the net from Hunt's perfectly judged lob over Gordon West's head.

6

My Hero

THE FOLLOWING season we finished sixth, just behind Liverpool in fifth. Manchester United won the league that year, and the following year their neighbours, Manchester City, did the same. I mention this only to underline the relief we all felt on the Blue side of the city that Liverpool didn't win anything. In fact, in 1968 Everton reached another FA Cup Final, this time against West Brom. It's a game that doesn't live in the memory – well, certainly not in mine, because we didn't win. We should have won on paper. Sadly, though, this football game wasn't played on paper.

On the day we were dreadful, which I blame on the fact we were playing in that dodgy yellow away kit. The game dragged on into a dreary period of extra time, when the West Brom centre-forward Jeff Astle – probably for first time in his career – scored with his left foot, completing the record of scoring in every round of the Cup.*

As a player Astle was known for his heading ability, scoring a significant portion of his 174 goals with his head. After his untimely death at fifty-nine years of age in 2002, a consultant neurologist told the inquest that Astle was suffering from a degenerative brain condition exacerbated by years of heading a football. In 2014 the campaign 'Justice for Jeff' was launched, calling for an independent inquiry into a possible link between dementia and heading footballs. Later that year it was confirmed that Astle was the first British player known to have died as a result of a career in football. Not everything about the old days was rosy.

The final season of the Sixties saw Everton reach the top again. We had a well-balanced group with strong players throughout the team, but there is no doubt that the engine room – the inspiration for our second

---

* After his career ended, Astle enjoyed another period of fame as a regular guest on *Football Fantasy* with David Baddiel and Frank Skinner. The fact that Skinner is a lifelong West Brom fan is purely coincidental.

league title of the decade – was our midfield trio of Howard Kendall, Colin Harvey and Alan Ball. Known later as 'the Holy Trinity' and honoured with a statue on Goodison Road, these three players formed an unbeatable partnership. Harvey, dubbed 'the white Pelé', was an elegant and skilful playmaker who was described during the 1968 Cup Final by the legendary commentator Kenneth Wolstenholme as 'a beautiful footballer'.

Alongside him was Kendall, a fierce tackler and winner of the ball, and the youngest player ever in an FA Cup Final (with Preston North End). A real crowd-pleaser was his trick of sliding into a hopeless tackle, clenching the ball in the crook of his leg without fouling the player, before jumping up with ball at his feet and smoothly passing to a teammate to set up an Everton attack. He was a world-class defensive half-back who should have been a regular in the England squad but bafflingly was never even capped. Of course, his time coincided with the World Cup-winning team and that midfield of Peters, Stiles, Charlton et al. But fringe players like Alan Mullery and Colin Bell were introduced as the 1960s turned into the 1970s, and the statistics would have shown that Kendall was easily as good if not better than them. No one paid attention to statistics in those days, though. It was probably a case of Kendall's face not fitting with Sir Alf Ramsey – a creature of habit who stuck loyally to his favoured group.

And then came Alan Ball to complete our trio. As soon as I saw Ball take to the pitch in the famous blue jersey with that stuttering run of his, I fell in love. What it is to have a hero when you're a prepubescent boy. Like me, he was ginger and unnecessarily – sometimes comically – belligerent. And, at only five foot six tall, he was not much taller than my eleven-year-old self. I wanted to be Alan Ball. When he sported his trademark white boots for the first time, I (along with thousands of young Everton fans) went straight out and bought a pair. No one bats an eyelid now when the modern footballer-cum-fashion icon prances onto the pitch wearing electric-blue footwear, but Ball's white boots were a new thing in 1969. Until that point, a bit like Henry Ford's Model T cars, you could have any colour as long as it was black. The white boots drew criticism from some of the more conservative parts of the football world, and that was just the way Ball liked it.

He was an immediate favourite with the crowd. We loved him and he loved us. He said so: 'Once Everton has touched you, nothing is the same.' You might think this is just a cynical trope by a player who is only pretending to be loyal. In recent years we've become inured to phoney shows of undying loyalty by multi-millionaire players patting their badges after scoring a goal, only to piss off after one season for a bigger payday overseas. But I believe Ball loved playing for Everton and was devastated when manager Harry Catterick sold him to Arsenal the year after he had been instrumental in us lifting the First Division trophy in May 1970. Only nine months earlier Catterick, when asked how much he thought Ball was worth, quoted the price of a million pounds, adding that he probably wouldn't sell him even at that price. Yet, within just twelve months, Catterick had sold him – and for £220,000. Why am I so confident that Ball didn't want to go to Arsenal? I asked him forty-five years later.

In 2006 I'd been invited by Peter Fincham, then Controller of BBC One, to watch England play their first group match in the World Cup hosted by Germany. We arrived at the stadium in time for lunch and were taken to the BBC section in a compound where the world's broadcast networks had set up camp to cover the tournament. Sitting at an outdoor lunch table were Gary Lineker and his fellow pundit Alan Shearer.

I knew Gary and said hello, briefly exchanged pleasant-ries with Shearer and then left Peter to talk to his stars because I had spotted someone who made my legs go a little wobbly: minding his own business at the far end of the table was my boyhood hero, Alan Ball. He was the BBC's special guest for the occasion, and there he was in living colour just in front of me. I instinctively looked at his feet, a little disappointed to see he wasn't wearing his white boots.

I realised I was nervous. In my line of work I meet a lot of famous people and I'm not usually affected by it. And, in truth, Alan Ball wasn't famous in that sense in 2006 – he could walk down most streets and not be recognised. But it wasn't his fame that made my stomach flip, it was the thought that I was about to talk to my boyhood hero. For a moment I was that sixteen-year-old boy again, the age I was when Ball left Everton. Usually a hard-bitten media type, I found myself tongued-tied and self-consciously staring at this small middle-aged man in a garden chair.

I introduced myself and told him I was a huge fan. He smiled benignly. 'I even bought the white boots,' I said, immediately regretting it. *What kind of twat says that*? I thought. More kind smiles. 'And when they sold you on 23 December in 1971, I cried all through Christmas and into the New Year.' I couldn't stop talking now. I'd lost all restraint. He stopped smiling, put down his cup of tea and said: 'Me too.' He explained: 'It wasn't a move I wanted but the club did, so I went.'

Forty-five years on, did I detect regret and a tinge of bitterness in that distinctive high-pitched Lancastrian voice? Players back then – even those as brilliant and feted as Alan Ball – were still the indentured employees of their clubs. The Bosman ruling in 1995 was to tip the balance in favour of the player, allowing him to leave his club at the end of his contract and become a free agent. By 2000 the popularity of the Premier League, supercharged by lucrative television deals and the advent of independent football agents, promoted the personal power of the players, especially the star performers. The talent was now calling the shots, not the men in suits. Ball and his generation missed out on that. I've met some other old Everton players in the hospitality suites on matchday who find it hard to understand what the modern footballer has to complain about with their astronomical salaries and huge mansions. Do some of these heroes of yesteryear feel they missed out? Of course they do. Are some bitter? A few, I suppose. Although, to a man, they always say playing professional football at the highest level and playing it at Everton was an absolute privilege.

I realise that some of my observations may come across as those of a grumpy old man. I am old, that's true, but I'm not grumpy. I still love watching football, but I regret that the love of money (didn't someone say it was the root of all evil?) now dominates the sport. I dislike the way clubs feed off the undying loyalty of fans, constantly issuing new kits, vintage kits, hoodies, baseball caps, and a ridiculous array of other merchandise aimed at children and doting parents, some of whom stretch themselves to afford the ever-increasing ticket prices. I cannot think it does the players any good to be dragged across the world for meaningless tournaments in the pursuit of further income. Yet, despite my misgivings about the foreign ownership of our national sport, and the obsession with money, and the league's slavish obedience to their television overlords, I still love the game itself. And I especially still love watching Everton – even more so when I watch it with my sons and uncle.

Now, let me gingerly step down from this soapbox and take you back to the 1970s.

7

Everton and I
Both Go Off

MANY SAW the sale of Ball as a defining moment in the club's history. Everton were one of the teams poised to dominate the scene in the 1970s, but selling Ball heralded a steady decline that would persist until the early 1980s. Ball wasn't just a great player, he took the team to a whole other level. Everton sold him in 1971 and wouldn't win another trophy for thirteen years. On paper, the decision to sell him was perfectly rational: Catterick had had five years of Ball in his prime (although he was still only in his mid-twenties) and received in transfer fees exactly twice what he had paid for him. But there is very little that is rational about the world of football, and if all you're considering is the return on investment and the bottom line, then you're in the wrong business. While the Ball deal may have doubled the return on investment, on the pitch it was a disaster.

The fact that the 1970s was a dismal period for the Blues was made even worse by the spectacular rise of Liverpool. In 1979 Liverpool won their fifth First Division championship of the decade and we finished one place above the relegation zone. Catterick had retired as manager in 1973, followed by the former player Billy Bingham and then Gordon Lee. Across the park, in 1974 sixty-year-old Bill Shankly retired after Liverpool had beaten Newcastle in that year's FA Cup Final. For a moment, the Blue side of the city breathed a sigh of relief, praying Liverpool might now do what most clubs do after an iconic manager leaves: wander off into the wilderness for a decade or so. But no, Shankly handed over to his number two, Bob Paisley, who irritatingly added a trophy for every one of the nine years he was in charge. The only solace I take from this is that Shankly ended up being made to feel less than welcome at his old club as his presence was deemed to be undermining Paisley (of whom he said: 'I could have left a monkey in charge' – classy). Another pleasing footnote for Evertonians is that Shankly claimed to have always been given a warmer welcome by the board of Everton when he attended a match at Goodison Park than by the board at Anfield. Perhaps Everton's board had not been shouted at and threatened by the irascible Scot with a messiah complex for nearly twenty years.

During this dismal period, my life changed dramatically. In 1974 I left my home in Walton to take a place at Jesus College, Cambridge, where I read Classics. My dad was thrilled that I had done well at school. He was a highly intelligent man who had to leave school at fourteen. He once said to me: 'There are two ways of making it in this city: football or education. I've seen you play football. Get yourself an education.'

As a boy I had attended my local school, Alsop Comprehensive. I liked school; in contrast to my home, it was regulated and reliable.* It was there that I met a

---

* Fun fact: in 1971 a cool, young French student teacher spent two terms at our school, researching his undergraduate thesis. He was football-mad and spent more time coaching the various football teams than writing his thesis. His name? Gérard Houllier. Yes, that one. When he returned to the city twenty-seven years later to coach the other lot, he remembered his time at Alsop in an interview with the *Liverpool Echo*, saying he was researching education in deprived areas. Thanks, Gérard. I had no idea I was deprived.

gifted Classics teacher called Douglas Cashin. He had spotted that I and my best friend, David Hughes, were good at Latin and encouraged us to take Ancient Greek. By A-level year we were in a class of three boys in a huge comprehensive in one of the more deprived areas of the city, reading the works of Euripides and Virgil in the original texts. Under Mr Cashin's guidance, David and I both applied to Cambridge and were accepted. I was heading off into my adult life far from my roots, and I couldn't wait to escape from Walton and from my family. I loved my parents, but I didn't like the chaos of a home dominated by alcoholism – my mother's in particular. When she was sober my mum was the kindest and most generous of women but, with a few ciders and gin and tonics down her, she became a different person. I remember a man at a family party saying to her once: 'You could start a row in an empty house.' So off I went to university, intending to reinvent myself and put Liverpool in my rear-view mirror.

I'm ashamed now to say that while I was at university I tried to minimise my trips home, and consequently I didn't see Everton play at home as I had done for the previous fifteen years. Of course, I would always check the results to see how we were doing, but I couldn't say

I saw them more than a handful of times during those years. I would call my mum and dad a couple of times a week, and they would visit me occasionally, but I felt very detached from my old life.

My father had always been particularly interested in my education and – despite his shift working hours and his fondness for the pub – he never missed a parents' evening, so when it was time for my final exams I rang home every night to tell him. My mother answered the phone on each occasion during those two weeks and would say that dad was working or he had gone out or some other reason he couldn't come to the phone. I was so self-involved with my exams – and just generally self-involved – that I didn't think anything of it. When, after my last exam, I excitedly told my mum that I had finished and would never have to take another exam ever again, she broke down at the other end of the phone. She said my father was in hospital, paralysed by some mystery virus almost at the same time as I had started my exams, but he had made her promise not to tell me until my exams were over. Thankfully the paralysis abated and my father came out of hospital, but he was terribly weak, in constant neurological pain, and now unable to work. Tate & Lyle, where he had been a boiler operator, had a generous pension scheme but my father liked to work. His illness robbed him of his vitality and his desire to meet up with his mates in The Hermitage. He loved to laugh, but he didn't laugh much now. Instead he was stuck at home with a father-in-law he didn't like and a wife whose drinking worsened.

I left Cambridge in 1977 and moved to London. I knew I wanted to be an actor, having been part of the acting and comedy fraternity at university. I had been in Footlights and that summer had appeared in their Edinburgh revue directed by Griff Rhys Jones. So I wrote to every repertory theatre in the country, asking for a job as a stage manager. These theatres, which employed a troupe of actors all year round, putting on new plays every three weeks, don't exist in the same way today as they did in the 1970s. I wrote to all of them. I got one reply, from The Marlowe Theatre in Canterbury, saying no. I had no job and nowhere to live, but David Hughes offered me a room in a house that he and some college friends were renting in Catford. I had no money at all and so there was no option: I would have to sign on.

I couldn't tell my parents. My family were working class – with the emphasis on 'working'. 'Work or want' was the mantra in my childhood home. So it was with some sense of failure and shame that I took my place in line at the Catford Employment Exchange. Eventually I reached the counter, where a middle-aged woman was scribbling on a form. She looked up and said: 'What kind of job are you looking for?'

'Ideally I'd like to be a film star,' I replied.

'There's not much call for that in Catford, but they're looking for porters in Lewisham Hospital.'

'I'll take it.'

A few months into my career as porter I received a call from Ian Davidson, who said he was a script editor at the BBC working on *The Two Ronnies*. He was putting together a new sketch show, had seen the Footlights Edinburgh revue I had appeared in, and wondered whether I would like to meet. Ian was very encouraging and commissioned me to write some sketches. Things were looking up.

Then one afternoon I was at the house in Catford, and the phone rang. The voice at the other end sounded sombre. It was a friend of the family: 'It's about your dad, Jimmy, I'm so sorry.' I was stunned and confused – my dad was infirm but his illness wouldn't have killed him. I asked: 'Did he kill himself?' Silence, and then: 'I'll explain when you get home.'

My father took his own life on 9 May 1978, nine days before his forty-ninth birthday. He had hanged himself at home, where my mum found him when she returned from work that day. This was the man who had given me Everton; his shoulders were the shoulders on which I perched as we walked to Goodison when I was a tiny boy. And now he was gone. I never wanted to go home again. How could I go to a game, knowing that he couldn't?

And so I immersed myself in my London life. In the early 1980s I got my Equity card and was working as a radio and television producer and sometimes as an actor. My mother would visit on the odd weekend, but it was awkward and painful. I would meet her at Euston, and she would often stumble out of the train drunk and have to be helped by some fellow passenger. We couldn't talk about what had happened when we were sober, but after a few drinks the tears and the anger would come out, often directed at each other, and then the following morning we would act like nothing had been said.

I hated my mother's drinking but I hadn't yet noticed that mine was getting worse.

8

Glory Days

THE 1970s turned into the 1980s and Everton were going nowhere. In 1981 we finished fifteenth, Toxteth was on fire and Margaret Thatcher had the nerve to wear blue. It was a depressing time. In the May that year our chairman, the gentlemanly Sir Philip Carter, sacked manager Gordon Lee. Lee had been at the club for five forgettable years. Enter Howard Kendall.

Kendall was already a legend at Everton and had been in the team the last time we won the league. Now he was back at Goodison as manager. His mission was clear but seemed impossible. In his first three seasons, we finished eighth and seventh twice. For most clubs this would be seen as steady progress, but we were only half a mile from one of the best teams in Europe and they were on a roll, winning three consecutive First Division championships in 1982, '83 and '84. We were mediocre by comparison, and when we hit rock bottom in November 1982 – after a 5-0 defeat in the Merseyside derby at Goodison Park – there were calls for Kendall to go. The 1983/84 season wasn't panning out any better, and by the new year it seemed that if Kendall couldn't put a cup run together he'd be out.

We were still in the League Cup (or the Milk Cup, as it was named for its sponsors at that point, the Milk Marketing Board) and had progressed to the quarter-finals, where we were up against Third Division Oxford at their ground. On their way to the quarter-finals they had beaten Newcastle, Leeds and Manchester United, so they were no pushover. I decided to travel up to Oxford to see them – I hadn't been to Goodison much since my dad died, but a quick trip up the M40 was manageable. Oxford played well and it was only Neville Southall in goal who kept the score to 0-0 at the break. Then the inevitable happened: Oxford took a deserved lead in the sixty-eighth minute. As the minutes ticked by, Oxford grew in confidence. I could see the headlines the following day: KENDALL SACKED! We needed a miracle…

It's at moments like this I think there might be a god, and it might be an Evertonian. Let me introduce Oxford midfielder Kevin Brock – Everton's Man of the Match that night. With less than ten minutes of the Kendall era remaining, poor Brock – who had played well throughout the match – attempted a simple back-pass to his keeper, unaware that our most prolific goalscorer, Adrian Heath, was lurking nearby. Heath intercepted the pass, took it around the keeper and equalised. The following week we beat them 4-1 at Goodison, got past Aston Villa in the semis, and now all we had to do was win the final. That would be, of course, against Liverpool.

The final was at 3 p.m. on Sunday 25 March. My old friend Peter Bennett-Jones, a tolerable Liverpool fan, and I had decided to go together and we met before the game at midday in The Dome, a trendy bar in Hampstead. We were both a little hungover from an excessive Saturday night and were nursing restorative Bloody Marys, when suddenly Peter's face drained of colour and he passed out. An ambulance was called and rushed him to the nearby Royal Free Hospital. He had regained consciousness and thankfully seemed to be in no danger. He told me I should go to the game. I didn't feel it was the right thing to do but he insisted, assuring me he was in good hands and saying it would be a shame to waste such sought-after tickets. Peter is a generous soul and placed his ticket in my hand and wished me well. I arrived at Wembley and decided to give the spare ticket to a Liverpool fan. I tried for some time to give it away to any one of the many fans who had come down to London without a ticket, but no one would take it from me. What was the catch? I was wearing a blue and white scarf and trying to give a free ticket to a passing Liverpool fan. Some recoiled as if the ticket was doused in Novichok; others looked around for a hidden camera. It was getting near kick-off time, so I changed my pitch from: 'Do you want a free ticket?' to: 'Wanna buy a ticket?' Success! (Though the buyer was still slightly suspicious that I only wanted the face value.)

It was a dreary, tense game – like many Merseyside derbies. Liverpool had the better chances, and again Southall was our saviour, but the referee Alan Robinson waved away a clear-cut penalty when Alan Hansen blatantly used his hand to steer away Adrian Heath's shot off the Liverpool goal line. The Wembley final finished 0-0, and then Liverpool won the replay at Maine Road 1-0.

Despite this setback, Kendall and Everton were ending the season well, and in May 1984 Everton were back at Wembley for the FA Cup Final against Elton John's Watford. I managed to get a couple of tickets and went to Wembley with my new stepfather, John, whom mum had married two years after my father's death. Fortunately, he was an Evertonian so there was no awkwardness on that front. A man of few words, on Wembley Way John trod on an upturned nail that pierced his shoe and became embedded in his foot. It was clearly painful, so I offered to help him get it out. He refused, saying it would only make it bleed more, so he left it there until we got home after the game. He was a man who didn't like to make a fuss. We had also both had quite a few drinks, which no doubt took the edge off. The result also took his mind off the searing pain: Everton won 2-0, with the first goal coming from our marauding Scottish centre-forward Graeme Sharpe and then a controversial second from our signing from Aston Villa, another Scot, Andy Gray. There was a moment of doubt about the Gray header as it was thought he had dislodged the ball illegally with his head from the goalkeeper's hands, but there was no VAR in 1984, so the referee gave the goal and we all went nuts. Our first trophy in fourteen years!

None of realised as we danced home from Wembley – some of us with bits of rusty metal in our feet – that we were on the threshold of Everton's most successful period in our club's history. Had we lost to Oxford five months earlier, Kendall would have gone and we would have gone into freefall. As it was, our manager had come through it, climbed a steep learning curve and found his best eleven – a strong, balanced, talented team. Thank you, Kevin Brock of Oxford.

The following season led some of us to believe we were again in a time of miracles. We won the league. And we didn't just win it – we walked it, finishing on ninety points, thirteen points clear of Liverpool in second place, and wrapping the title up with five games to play. We were also in the FA Cup Final against a shaky Manchester United managed by mahogany-tanned wide boy Ron Atkinson. And if that wasn't enough, we had reached the final of the European Cup Winners' Cup – the treble was on! The team was heralded as the best in the land. The players even enjoyed the dreadful rite of passage of recording a jaunty football song, 'Here We Go', which reached number fifteen in the charts and had them signing it on *Wogan*. Everton had arrived.

It seemed Kendall had finally got the team he wanted, both on and off the pitch. He had brought in Colin Harvey to be first-team coach. Harvey had played alongside Kendall and Ball in that league-winning team and had already managed the reserve team. He knew the good young players coming through and had incredibly high standards. The two former teammates were back in lockstep.

Certain tweaks had been made to the previous year's cup-winning squad. Pat Van Den Hauwe was added at left-back just after the beginning of the season. In interviews Pat had a compelling and almost disturbing stillness about him, as if he had seen terrible things of which he dared not speak. Fittingly nicknamed 'Psycho', he could look after himself and his teammates; he was the kind of guy you wanted inside your tent. The talented midfielder Paul Bracewell, a fantastic passer of the ball, joined from Sunderland to complete the group. There was no star, no huge figure who stood out from this team. We had the immense Neville Southall in goal who, like many of his kind, was a big character and almost impossible to get past. Anchoring a solid defence, we had captain Kevin Ratcliffe, a local lad and lifelong Evertonian who said that as a boy he'd only ever dreamed of playing for Everton at Goodison. Trevor Steven on the right wing was clever and elegant. Adrian 'Inchy' Heath up front couldn't stop scoring. And at the centre of it all, playing as passionately with his mouth as he did with his feet, was our very own Napoleon: Peter Reid – a man who would shed blood for Everton, preferably someone else's. As individuals they were talented, but as a team they were perfect. Balanced, resilient and great to watch, they played *for* each other and looked *after* each other. It was a band of brothers. Suddenly we felt like an outfit that could take on the 'Red Shite'.

I should make special mention of Heath because of what happened to him halfway through that season. He had been our top scorer the previous year and was tipped to gain a place in Bobby Robson's England squad. Just before Christmas 1984, his campaign ended when his anterior cruciate ligament was torn as a result of a dangerous tackle by the Sheffield Wednesday winger Brian Marwood. Heath was out for nine months and would miss out on the European Cup Winners' Cup and the FA Cup Final. He was at Goodison when we lifted the league trophy, but even when he recalled that time in a recent interview – several decades later – the regret and pain were still near the surface. On a brighter note, later in that fateful game Reid hammered Marwood, and hammered him every time we played Sheffield Wednesday thereafter. As I said, this team looked after each other.

The 1984/85 season was crowned with our winning the European Cup Winners' Cup, for which we had qualified by winning the previous year's FA Cup. We dominated a one-sided final against a mediocre Rapid Wien, running out 3-1 winners with goals from Trevor Steven, Kevin Sheedy and Andy Gray, who had stepped in for Heath and was scoring for fun. But the final is not the game that Evertonians still talk about. The game that is relived and still drooled over is the semi-final second leg against Bayern Munich at Goodison Park. It is remembered as the greatest night of football at Goodison Park.

The first leg had been a 0-0 draw, so it was all to play for that night in April 1985. Despite Everton's home advantage, Bayern were favourites to win, having just thrashed Roma 4-1 in the quarter-finals. The game started brightly, with Everton having much of the play. The tackles were flying in, and neither side was giving quarter. Our skipper Kevin Ratcliffe said in the brilliant Everton documentary *Howard's Way*: 'If you look back at the game now, it should be X-rated. Anybody under twelve shouldn't be allowed to watch it.' Even by Goodison standards, the atmosphere was – in the words of the great poet Martin Tyler – 'a cacophony of noise'. But the crowd was suddenly silenced in the thirty-eighth minute when, against the run of play, Dieter Hoeness put Bayern ahead.

At half-time Kendall kept calm and kept his message simple. According to Peter Reid, he said: 'Get the ball in the box. The Gwladys Street end will suck it in.' Not the sort of tactic you'd expect Pep Guardiola or Arne Slot to point to on their iPads these days, but it worked: within three minutes of the restart, Everton were back in it. Gray flicked a long Gary Stevens throw-in on to Graeme Sharpe, who gratefully nodded it past the Bayern goalkeeper, Jean-Marie Pfaff, for an equaliser. Soon afterwards, Gray scored from another long throw after Pfaff had fumbled. It was a classic goalie error, probably a crucial turning point in the game, and probably the last thing the poor man sees every night as he slips into a heavily medicated sleep. But still we weren't done, and the game was crowned with a well-worked move as Gray again laid it off to Trevor Steven, who clipped it past our old friend Pfaff to make it 3-1.

This night is regarded as the greatest in the club's history. Andy Gray – a man not known for his lack of something to say – said of it: 'If you talk to any Evertonian who was there that night, and you said, "You can take one game to the grave with you." Say there was 55,000 people, I'm betting you 50,000 would take this game with them.' Well, *I* wouldn't. Well, I *couldn't* as I wasn't there!

As I mentioned, my attendance at Goodison Park was virtually non-existent at that time. I was now living and working in London as a full-time actor, appearing on Channel 4's topical sketch show *Who Dares Wins*. I was drinking a bit too much and about 1983 had decided that taking cocaine on a regular basis would be a splendid idea, so to say life was unmanageable and chaotic would be accurate. I have no idea why I didn't go to the game – I can't remember, although there is a lot I don't remember about the 1980s.

I do remember why I wasn't at the FA Cup Final against Manchester United three days after the European Cup Winners' game. It was Saturday 18 May, my father's birthday, and I was working at BBC Television Centre, producing the first series of *Alas Smith and Jones*, the new sketch series starring *Not the Nine*

O'Clock News alumni Griff Rhys Jones and Mel Smith. Wembley was only half an hour's drive away from the BBC but there was no hope of slipping off for three hours to catch the game. So I had a TV set wheeled to the props department at the side of the studio, meaning I could keep up with the game. We had thrashed United 5-0 earlier in the season, so we were favourites to lift the Cup and achieve the unprecedented treble of the two major domestic trophies and a European title.

Unfortunately, an Everton treble looked too good to be true and so it turned out. We didn't show up that day, and later there were rumours of too much celebrating after the Cup win three days earlier in Rotterdam. It was a miserable final, and at the end of ninety minutes no one had bothered the keepers. Then, well into extra time, Norman Whiteside – the United hardman, not known for his scoring prowess – deftly placed it out of reach of the usually reliable Southall and that was that: no treble. At that moment I had a brief insight of what it must be like for fans of one of the current top clubs whose expectations are so high that not completing a treble is felt – even momentarily – as a crushing defeat. It's a special kind of pain reserved for the overentitled. I see it sometimes on the face of a shopper in Wholefoods Kensington when they're told the shop has run out of oat milk.

The Wembley defeat was a blow but what happened eleven days later at a stadium in Brussels would overshadow that and the whole of English football for the next five years. On 29 May Liverpool were to play Juventus at the Heysel Stadium in the European Cup Final. Before the game a group of Liverpool fans thought it would be a good idea to breach a neutral zone and charge at the Juventus fans, who panicked and tried to escape the enclosure. The stadium was old, and a crumbling perimeter wall collapsed, leading to hundreds of injuries and the deaths of thirty-nine fans, most of them Italian. Fourteen Liverpool fans were later convicted of manslaughter and UEFA banned all English clubs from Europe for five years, Liverpool for six.

The Heysel disaster is not much discussed these days. There was another stadium disaster about to happen in 1989 – an avoidable tragedy involving Liverpool fans, who this time would be the victims of an unsafe Hillsborough stadium, criminally incompetent policing, and much more in the subsequent cover-up by the corrupt authorities who for years disgracefully blamed the fans. So perhaps it's understandable that the Heysel incident has slightly faded from memory on Merseyside. But the name 'Heysel' is inscribed on the hearts and minds of every Everton fan of that vintage. This five-year ban inflicted on all clubs was seen as monumentally unfair because, along with Liverpool, Everton had been the most dominant force in the First Division and were looking at a sustained period of lucrative European football that no doubt would have prepared us well to take our place at the top table in the Premier League in 1992. The fact that this prospect had been taken from us by a handful of supporters of our neighbour and keenest rival did not go unnoticed.

9

The End of an Era

THE FOLLOWING year, as the 1985/86 season drew to a close, the two Merseyside teams were again going head to head for both the First Division title and the FA Cup. By the time the last Saturday of the season came round, both teams were in the FA Cup Final, and Everton were only two points behind Liverpool in the league. We had a game in hand against West Ham the following Monday, so we needed Liverpool to lose at Chelsea and us to beat Southampton and West Ham, both at Goodison.

You would have thought for this, the most important day in the club's year, I'd have gone to see them in the flesh. You'd be wrong. Instead, I decided to take my young brother John to see Chelsea play Liverpool. John was a Liverpool fan. His father was an Everton fan but had never taken him to a match – unlike his uncle, who unfortunately was Red. Shit happens. John was keen to see if his team could win the league, and I was keen to see if they couldn't.

I watched the game at Stamford Bridge with a transistor radio clamped to my ear for the score at Goodison Park. I felt more than a pang of guilt and shame that I was in the wrong stadium. I wasn't making the best decisions in my life during this period, and this had been one of the worst. The game at Goodison sounded amazing, and incredibly we beat Southampton 6-1, with Gary Lineker – who we'd signed from Leicester at the beginning of the season – scoring a hat-trick and bringing his season's tally up to thirty league goals.

So at Goodison we had done the impossible and now had a better goal difference than our rivals. All Chelsea had to do was hold Liverpool to a draw. Could they do it? Of course they couldn't. This was the 1980s, when Chelsea were a nice family club but a shit football team. Kenny Dalglish, Liverpool's player-manager, scored the only goal of the game and broke my heart at Stamford Bridge.

There was hope of revenge the following Saturday, when we were to meet the new champions at Wembley in the FA Cup Final. I was there again with my Liverpool-supporting little brother, who had wisely kept his mouth shut in the week since his team's win. Wembley was bathed in sunshine, and both Blue and Red Scousers together filled the national stadium for the second time this decade, singing as one to taunt their common enemy: 'Are you watching, Manchester?' Again the referee was Alan Robinson, who hadn't given us that clear Hansen penalty at the Milk Cup Final in 1984, and when his name was called over the PA system we let him know we hadn't forgotten.

There had been speculation that this would be Lineker's last game at Everton. He had done well by us, scoring forty goals in all competitions and winning Footballer of the Year, but the word was that Barcelona were after him. Those rumours proved to be true, and Lineker left the club that summer. Understandably, he wanted European football, and neither Everton nor any other English club could give him that. However, he said goodbye in the best way possible: following up on a shot parried by Bruce Grobbelaar and tucking it away for a trademark close-range finish.

The second half was a different story. We had chances: Sharpe's looping header tipped over by the keeper; Sheedy's free-kick turned around the post by the excellent Grobbelaar; Lineker uncharacteristically not chasing down a loose ball in front of goal. Liverpool had their chances too, but they took every one of theirs: first Ian Rush, then Craig Johnston and finally Rush again. The inevitability of it all was depressing. Rush – like a few Anfield legends – apparently started life as an Everton fan; there was no sign of his former affiliation that day. The worst thing at the end of the game was having to sit there and watch Liverpool fans wallow in their victory. As I recall, the Everton fans stoically stayed until the bitter end for the presentation of the losers' and winners' medals and the raising of the cup. If you're an Everton fan, you know how to lose – and in those seven days in May 1986 we had plenty of practice.

That autumn, smarting from the previous season's hurt, Kendall set about restoring dignity at Goodison and duly won the league in May 1987 – his second title in three years. From 1984 to 1987 he won four major trophies, including a European title, making him the most successful manager in Everton's history, but now he was off. Frustrated by the ban from Europe (this was the second season we had missed out on a European campaign due to the Heysel ban), in the summer of 1987 Kendall moved to Spain to manage Athletic Bilbao. He had given thousands of Evertonians unbridled joy in those years, and many hours of reminiscing ever since, but that was that: the end of an era. But what an era it was.

10

A Flirtation

I HAVE a confession to make: I was unfaithful to Everton in the late 1980s. On an impulse I decided to get two season tickets at the newly promoted Wimbledon FC. I told myself that I lived in nearby Wandsworth, that I loved football, that Wimbledon would host First Division games, that I would see Everton play them once a year... I am both a good salesman and very gullible, so I can convince myself of anything. The second ticket was for my younger brother, John, who had moved down from Liverpool at the age of twelve, when his father's and my mother's drinking got worse.

Like any dalliance, my flirtation with Wimbledon didn't last. During that season I realised, as the unfaithful are bound to do, that the grass is not greener.

It certainly wasn't greener at Plough Lane, where the pitch cut up badly. Yes, there was something cool and quirky about going along to watch the Crazy Gang. They were the underdogs who punched above their weight and whose manager Dave Bassett is to be applauded for bringing them up from Division Four to the top division in five years. Besides, who doesn't want to see a rabid Vinnie Jones exact terrifying violence on a Manchester United player? But it wasn't like watching Everton – apart from the one game when Wimbledon played Everton, of course. I just couldn't get that excited as a neutral, though. I loved watching football, and some games were entertaining, but at Wimbledon I was an interested observer rather than a fan. I missed the elation and the despair, the joy and the misery that only comes from watching the team you love.

I was still debating whether to continue spending every other Saturday at Plough Lane when fate intervened and decided for me. John and I had seats in the family enclosure, which I assumed would be far enough away from the lunatics to be safe. The Saturday in question, Wimbledon were up against Southampton. The visitors had a talented winger called Danny

Wallace, one of the few Black players in the First Division at the time. Seated in front of us was a man with a young boy of perhaps six or seven on his knee. He was the kind of man who thinks everyone needs to hear his opinion. Every time Wallace got the ball, this twat made monkey noises and gestures, and after a while the young boy joined in. I could see that the non-morons sitting nearby were becoming increasingly uncomfortable. What baffled me was that John Fashanu was playing up front for Wimbledon and elicited no such noises from the idiot seated in front of us. Clearly his racism was inconsistent.

I was not known for keeping my cool in those days and was bursting to give this guy a mouthful, but I was also – and still am – a physical coward, and this racist lump in front of me was big so I decided to take my complaint to the steward who was watching the game from the back of the small wooden stands. Surely the club would have rules about this kind of behaviour. I edged out of my seat and told the steward that someone was shouting out racist abuse. Irritated that I was distracting him from his main job of watching the match, he asked me who it was. I pointed to the beer belly on legs with the child on his lap. 'Oh,' he said laughing, 'that's just Frank. He's only having a bit of fun. He means no harm.'

I looked at the steward, whose gaze had gone back to the match, and realised that there were better things to do on a Saturday.

11

The Good Times Are Over

Everton ended the 1980s with a whimper. I did the same, stumbling into a rehab facility in December 1988. I stayed for three months, admitting to myself that I was an alcoholic and an addict. In the January, my mother came to visit and sat in what was called the Family Group, a meeting in which family members could tell their relative in treatment what it had been like to witness their loved one's descent into addiction. We started every meeting by going around the room and saying who we were and why we there. When it came to me, I simply said that I was Jimmy, an alcoholic and addict in treatment here. My mother was sitting next to me, looking nervous. When she was sober my mum was shy, anxious and beyond generous. She said:

'My name is June, I'm an alcoholic and I'm Jimmy's mum.' I was stunned. I knew she was an alcoholic – I'd told her often enough – but to hear those words leave her mouth was extraordinary. I was speechless and very happy. She told me later that John, her husband, had got help the year before and stayed sober, so a few months later she had followed his example and now she was sober too. On that day my mum and I started a new relationship which lasted for thirty-three years until she died in 2022, still sober.

Being newly clean and sober in the early 1990s as an Everton supporter gave me plenty of opportunities to test the strength of my recovery. If ever I was going to go back on the drink it would have been then. Colin Harvey had taken the baton from Kendall and expectations had been high. His credentials could not have been better: legendary club player, successful coach of the reserve team bringing on younger players, excellent first-team coach alongside Kendall. On paper he was the right appointment, but the big job didn't suit him. Everton were not going to have the same succession story that Liverpool enjoyed after Shankly left. We had drifted into mid-table mediocrity and by October 1990 had slumped dangerously to eighteenth in the league, having only won one of our first ten games. Sir Philip Carter sacked Harvey and brought Kendall back for a second stint. Everton fans were delighted. Hope came back to Goodison Park – hope that the good times were coming back – but we all know what a lying bastard hope is. Kendall had ditched Manchester City, where he had been manager for less than a year, saying: 'Manchester City was an affair. Everton was a marriage.' Maybe he should have talked to a couples' therapist before coming back to his 'wife'; perhaps they would have told him a lot of marriages don't do well after one of the partners has had an affair.

And so it was with the Everton/Kendall recoupling. Yes, he got us up the table in his first season back, but it wasn't the same. He was no longer the magician who conjured up league trophies, unforgettable European nights and scoring for fun. The Premier League, created at the beginning of the 1992/93 season, saw a shift of power. The city of Liverpool was no longer the centre of the footballing universe; that had relocated to Manchester and more specifically Old Trafford. United won the league eight times in the Premier League's first decade, interrupted only by Alan Shearer (otherwise known as Blackburn Rovers) and then Arsenal under their new manager, Arsène Wenger. Our only consolation as Evertonians was that Liverpool didn't win anything in those first few years of the Premier League.* Kendall's attempt to rekindle his 'marriage' with Everton ended dismally, and he left in December 1993 amid rumours of disagreements with the board. We were a mid-table club by then and we hated it. Little did we know that thirty years later we'd dream of the giddy heights of being twelfth in the league.

Enter the next contestant in the Make Everton Great Again competition: Mike Walker. Walker had received some media attention by surprisingly taking Norwich to third place in the first season of the Premier League. Building on that success, he took Everton to seventeenth the following year, avoiding relegation by two points. In a laudable act of faith, Everton stuck with him for the beginning of the 1994/95 season, but by November we were rooted to the foot of the table without a single win in our first twelve matches. Faith was

---

* Actually they won the League Cup in 1995, but that doesn't count. Who can take a cup seriously that has been called the Milk Cup, Littlewoods Cup, Rumblelows Cup, Coca-Cola Cup, Worthington Cup, Carling Cup, Capital One Cup, and the Carabao Cup? What's next? The YouPorn Cup?

replaced by reality, and Walker was dismissed. He must have been missing Delia Smith's pies because he went straight back to Norwich – just in time to take them down to the Championship at the end of that season.

Walker was swiftly replaced by our league-winning former centre-forward Joe Royle at the end of 1994 when we were looking up at the other twenty two clubs in the league. Could he get us off the bottom and into much-coveted mid-table mediocrity? Well, he certainly knew his way round the bottom of the Premier League, having taken Oldham down to the Championship just the year before. At least we didn't have to bother with finding any room for hope.

12

A Different Kind of Blue

MY DATING other clubs didn't end with my flirtation with Wimbledon. By 1990 I was splitting my days between acting and developing shows for our new production company. Denise O'Donoghue, Rory McGrath and I had set up Hat Trick in 1986, joined by Geoffrey Perkins a year later, and we were getting busy with returning shows like *Whose Line Is It Anyway?* and *Have I Got News for You*. Lots of great young writers and producers were in and out of the office; it was an exciting time. Andy Hamilton was making his mark as one of the country's top comedy writers, and would soon write one of Hat Trick's biggest hits of the 1990s, *Drop the Dead Donkey*, with Guy Jenkin. Andy had created, co-written and co-produced *Who Dares Wins* and was a regular visitor to the office. One day we were talking about football and I mentioned that Goodison was too far for me to go on a Saturday to watch Everton regularly, when Andy casually suggested that I could join him and his dad, Jim, and go to Stamford Bridge to watch Chelsea. It seemed like a perfect solution: I was now living off the Fulham Road, about a twenty-minute walk to Stamford Bridge; I had convinced myself that going to Liverpool for the day every other Saturday was too difficult; and Chelsea played in blue, didn't they? So for the second time I opted to buy season tickets for a team that wasn't Everton, and for a couple of seasons John, who was now nineteen, and I became regulars at Stamford Bridge.

Matchdays with Andy and his dad were a high-light of the week: eating fish and chips in Jim's flat on Ifield Road, listening to Jim tell his stories while Andy gently teased him, and talking about the game during our stroll to the ground all felt so warm and natural. It reminded me of when I would do the same with my dad, although that was a long time ago now. It was a welcome few hours in the genial company of football lovers. A regular bunch of us would sit in the East Stand every home game. We were joined by Andy's cousin Johnny and an old friend, Dave. Just behind us sat two other regulars, Len and Dave, both fervent Chelsea fans who loved to do nothing more than to criticise their team, like any self-respecting fan.

We sat in a half-empty stand in a half-empty stadium. In 1992 you could wander up at five to three to the turnstile, where there was no queue, and you'd get any spot you liked. If you looked fit enough you might even have got a game. Local fans from the area around the stadium – like Andy, Jim, Dave, Johnny, Len and Dave who had been going to Chelsea their entire lives – attended every game, but that wasn't enough to fill the ground. Stamford Bridge had to wait for Roman's roubles before it could top up the stadium with a new kind of fan. The multigenerational working-class fans have been supplemented by the nouveau supporter, the kind of fan who calls football 'footie', refers to the players by their first names, and knows nothing of their team before the money was injected. Nowadays I imagine there's a fifty-year waiting list for a seat at Stamford Bridge. That is why now when we play Chelsea to a packed stadium, I enjoy the Everton fans singing: 'Where were you when you were shit?'

Like a few older Chelsea fans, I'm not a huge fan of the new Chelsea. Stamford Bridge feels very different these days and I've had a couple of nasty encounters there. In November 2007 I was taken as a guest into one of the posh lounges for Chelsea v Everton. My host and I were sitting in a fairly sedate section by the halfway line. Everton were 1-0 down. Chelsea had dominated and the last few minutes were winding down. Then a cross came in from Everton's right, it bounced up off a defender and Tim Cahill leapt acrobatically and bicycle-kicked the ball into the net. I didn't cheer. I didn't stand. I knew better. All I did was clap twice and said, 'great goal'. At that, two gentlemen in their sixties, dressed in sober suits and ties and who only a couple of hours earlier had been eating the same overcooked food as me in the lounge, turned around and stared at me: 'Do you support this Scouse scum, you cunt?' I pointed out that Cahill was, to be accurate, *Australian* scum but these two were in no mood for light banter. I watched them as they ranted incoherently, like a more intellectually challenged version of Statler and Waldorf from *The Muppet Show*, their faces growing purple, and then I suggested that maybe some anger management might be helpful. Note to self: don't suggest anger management to a man who is literally spitting with rage.

Chelsea's transformation from a London family club into a global brand is due to their twenty-year record of domestic and European success, which in turn is due to the massive injection of wealth from a Russian oligarch. They have gained vast amounts of silverware but sadly have also attracted a lot of undesirables. I comfort myself with the fact that up to now Everton have been so terrible they are unlikely to be bothered by the fair-weather fan. Having said all that, I'm very happy to remember my brief association with a Chelsea that no longer exists, and I am very grateful for Andy and his dad accompanying me in my strange 'blue' period. It was a fellowship of real football fans, and it was good fun, but it wasn't Everton. Maybe it was time to bite the bullet.

13

Saved by the Bill

I WAS still telling myself that Goodison was just too far to go on a Saturday, when fate intervened again.

I was still working as an actor in the early 1990s, and when I came out of the treatment centre I was offered a part in a brilliant play called *Valued Friends* at the Hampstead Theatre. It had a great cast – including a very young Martin Clunes, who stole the show as a hilariously pissed-off estate agent. The Liverpudlian writer Alan Bleasdale – who had created one of the landmark television series of the 1980s, *Boys from the Blackstuff*, a savage, and sometimes savagely funny, indictment of Thatcher's Britain – was a friend of our director, Robin Lefevre, and came to the show on a few occasions. Alan and I got on well, and later that year he offered me a part in his signature Channel 4 drama *G.B.H.* starring Robert Lindsay, Julie Walters and Michael Palin. Soon after that, my agent got a call from Bill Kenwright's office, asking me to a meeting with Bill. I knew Bill from afar; he had migrated from being an actor on *Coronation Street* to being one of the West End's most successful impresarios, but he was also a well-known Evertonian and had a seat on the club's board of directors.

'Alan Bleasdale told me he saw you in that play recently,' he said to me in the meeting. 'He has written a very funny play called *Having a Ball*. It's about a man who's had a vasectomy. Fancy being in it?'

I can't remember now why I didn't do the play. Maybe Bill or Alan had second thoughts or maybe I didn't fancy appearing on stage naked as the role required. But the more important point is that, out of the blue, he said: 'You're an Everton fan?' I confirmed that I was, and he asked: 'How often do you go up?'

'Not very often,' I replied, with a stab of guilt.

'Why not?'

Why was he turning into Jeremy Paxman? And why was I feeling so uncomfortable?

I stammered an unconvincing reply: 'I'm a bit

busy… and it's a long way on a weekend, you know, and… er…'

He cut me off: 'I'm busy too but I go to every home game. We're at home on Saturday. Meet me at Euston at 9.30 a.m. and I'll show you how easy it is.'

Not sure how to respond, I whimpered: 'OK.'

I was a couple of years sober now so could rely on myself to turn up. That Saturday I walked across Euston Station and met Bill and a cheerful, quietly spoken man who worked at Bill's theatre company, John Collinge. John handed me a train ticket and told me I was now a member of ESCLA, an acronym I never deciphered but which meant I was now part of some travelling Everton away supporters' club of which he was secretary and general organiser. There were about five in the group – plus Bill, who held court on the journey up, regaling us with stories of Everton nights of glory and disaster, and occasionally hinting conspiratorially at something tantalising said at a recent board meeting upon which he couldn't elaborate.

I enjoyed the trip up enormously. The train got us there in about two and a half hours, so I had time to pop in to see my mum and John for a cup of tea and then stroll up to the ground, watch the game – I forget who we were playing that day – get back on the train with Bill and the gang, analyse the match on the journey, and to my astonishment get home by 8.30 p.m. – less than twelve hours after setting off. Bill was right, it was easy.

I'd had a great day. In fact, I had enjoyed it so much that I didn't repeat the experience again for quite some time. What was wrong with me?

A year later I wasn't feeling great. By that point I was about three years away from the days of booze and coke, but I felt incredibly stuck. I now know that it's very common for people who get into recovery from addiction to experience a second rock bottom a few years into their sobriety. On the advice of my friend and mentor, Tim, I went to see someone. Like a lot of people, I didn't feel thrilled at the idea of going 'into therapy', but Tim had been to see him and that was a good enough recommendation.

The therapist, a Welshman called Bruce Lloyd, wasn't at all what I was expecting. I hadn't met anyone quite like him. In our first session, he sat and beckoned me to do the same opposite him. He stared at me for an uncomfortably long time before suddenly saying: 'What don't you like about all this so far?' I'd only been there two minutes. He said: 'Be honest.'

'OK. You're wearing sandals with socks, which I've always thought is weird. You're Welsh and, coming from Liverpool, I was raised to be suspicious of the Welsh. And a part of me thinks therapy is bullshit.'

He looked at me and smiled: 'Thank you for your honesty. Well, I can't do anything about being Welsh, I like wearing my Dr Scholl's with socks, and I agree some of this lark is bullshit. Shall we get started?'

I was in. I liked this bloke. He slightly threw me in that first session by asking me to promise not to kill myself in the first six weeks. I nodded, rather taken aback. How bad was this going to be? Well, it wasn't easy. He explained we would start as far back as I could remember and we would slowly retrace my steps up to the moment I embarked on the lost journey of active addiction.

After a few months we were in the middle of a session and suddenly Bruce raised his hand to indicate he wanted me to stop talking. 'Jimmy,' he said, moving his chair closer. (His chair was on castors, so he could quickly come alongside you for dramatic effect, like some mad Welsh Dalek. It could be disconcerting.) 'Jimmy,' he repeated (he loved repeating your name in a slightly lower octave, also for dramatic effect), 'it's time to go home.'

123

I didn't know what he meant. Was he throwing me out of his office? Had I completed the course? It didn't feel that way. I was in bits. No, Bruce explained that it was obvious to him that I'd been on the run from Liverpool and had tried to forget the original pain I'd first felt there – my father's suicide, my mother's drinking, all of it. The solution was difficult but simple, he said: I had to go back and reconnect with all of it.

But how? Having been up to Goodison now and again with Bill Kenwright, I could no longer use my excuse that it was impractical to go to Liverpool because it was too far; my membership of the ESCLA had put paid to that.

I was beginning to suspect that neither Liverpool nor my family were the problem. I was.

Something else happened around this time to confirm my suspicions. In 1993 I attended the Edinburgh TV Festival, where ground-breaking television writer Dennis Potter was giving the keynote James MacTaggart Memorial Lecture. Potter was dying of pancreatic cancer and was sipping a gin-and-morphine cocktail at the lectern. He began by saying he had called his tumour 'Rupert', after the owner of the *Sun* newspaper, and savaged Murdoch in the most hilarious way before going on to describe the director general of the BBC as a 'Dalek'. He clearly no longer cared about not biting the hand that fed him – maybe he never did – but then he adopted a gentler, more wistful tone and talked about his childhood as the son of a coal miner in the Forest of Dean. He said that when he was fourteen his English teacher at school had told him that if he worked hard, he could possibly get a state scholarship to Oxford. Potter told the audience he was excited by this prospect and readily agreed to it, and he feels that deal he made was in some ways a betrayal of where he had come from. I was stunned. He was talking both *to* me and *about* me; I had made that deal with the world, and standing there aged thirty-seven I felt a million miles from the place where I was formed. I felt dreadful.

14

The Way Back

EVERTON WERE bottom of the league in December 1994, and I was in Australia, trying to sell *Have I Got News for You* to an Australian broadcaster.* On hearing of my intended trip, my mother had told me to visit Uncle John (who was in fact her uncle, having been her mother's stepbrother), who had left Liverpool as a young man in the 1950s as a Ten Pound Pom and now lived in Dandenong, a suburb of Melbourne. Initially I was unenthusiastic. I was always reluctant to meet people my mother insisted I should meet, especially members of my wider family. I know Bruce Lloyd had said I needed to go back to Liverpool and reconnect

---

* Spoiler alert: I'm still trying.

with my family, but hadn't he heard of procrastination? Then my mother said a couple of things that changed my mind: she mentioned that John had been great pals with my dad, as he'd been in the navy like my dad, and that he supported Everton FC. 'I'll go,' I told her.

Uncle John turned out to be a lovely man. He had a strange Scouse Australian accent and, after a classic roast lunch, we spent the afternoon reminiscing about the times he and my dad had gone to Goodison and about the days John spent in Liverpool before emigrating. He told me he had visited Liverpool in 1975 when I was away at university, and to prove it he dug out some old Super 8 film with no sound, which he said he'd taken at one of the many impromptu parties at my house in Walton. He thought it had caught my father singing on camera, which seemed plausible as my father liked to sing at parties – songs like 'Are You Lonesome Tonight?' 'I Left My Heart in San Francisco', 'Danny Boy'.* John gave me the film, and when I got home I had it transferred immediately to VHS. I put it in the video player and, just as Uncle John had said,

---

* He could also recite the soliloquy of Mark Anthony over the dead body of his friend Julius Caesar from Shakespeare's play of the same name, but that's for a different book.

there was my father on the screen, silently mouthing some sentimental ballad to an appreciative and well-lubricated audience. It was the first time I had seen my father since his death seventeen years earlier. Now I watched him moving about silently, laughing, pointing to my mother, people applauding him. He was right in the middle of his life. I realised just how much I missed him and just how hard I had tried to ignore that fact.

A little while later I was asked to take part in a series on the BBC about grief, *The Long Goodbye*. I didn't want to do it at first, but again I turned to Tim for advice, and he told me to do it: 'Not enough people talk about grief, especially about suicide.' I agreed. The producers asked me if I had any photos of my dad. I told them I could do better than that, and gave them Uncle John's film.

Before I left John's house that day in Australia, I had said casually that if Everton ever got to the FA Cup Final, I'd bring him over and we'd go. His reply was: 'Jimmy, I'm so old and they're so shit, I'll be a long time dead before we get to Wembley again.' Five months later we were in the final against Manchester United.

I rang John after we had hammered Spurs 4-1 in the semis. I had heard that his wife, Pat, had had a stroke and so I told him that I could get tickets and organise his flight for the final but, given Pat's health, I would totally understand if he didn't want to come. I could hardly finish the sentence before he said: 'No, don't worry, the kids can look after her. I'm coming.'

I was living in a flat in Chelsea at the time and John was going to stay with me until after the game and then go up to Liverpool to see his brothers and my mum. On the afternoon of his arrival, he was watching television in the other room while I made him a cup of tea in the kitchen. I heard him shout out in surprise. He was old and so my first thought was that he'd fallen or he was ill, but when I charged into the room he was pointing at the television open-mouthed: 'I've just seen that piece of film I gave you in Australia on the telly.' I had forgotten all about my interview on *The Long Goodbye*. It had been a few months back and I didn't even know it was on that day. I explained what I had done. He was thrilled that his bit of home movie had just been on national television and that he just happened to be sitting there when it came on.

'What are the odds of that, Jimmy?'

'Probably about as long as the odds of us beating United on Saturday, Uncle John.'

Manchester United were clear favourites to beat us. They had finished only one point behind the champions that year, Blackburn Rovers, while we'd been lucky to finish fifteenth. Joe Royle leant into our underdog status. In fact, he wallowed in canine metaphor that year, coining our soubriquet, the Dogs of War.

I was excited to be at Wembley with Uncle John – a man I hardly knew but felt I'd known all my life. There was an easy familiarity and we shared a similar sense of humour and dread. We had decent seats, but I spent the match partly watching the game and partly watching my old uncle watch the game. Everton were under siege from the kick-off, though. Would this be another disappointing day at Wembley?

Half an hour in, Everton broke from defence and moved the ball upfield quickly to Graham Stuart, who clattered it against the bar. It looped into the air, and our centre-forward, Paul Rideout, leapt up to nod it past Peter Schmeichel. 1-0 to Everton with an hour to go. Ten years previously we had been favourites and lost 1-0 to the underdogs, Manchester United; today it was the other way round. Would the football gods favour us this time? It was a long sixty minutes – and no doubt our goalkeeper, Neville Southall, kept us in it – but as the minutes ticked by, hope grew within the Everton ranks. So did the tension. I kept checking on Uncle John – I was worried this was all too stressful for him, and I didn't want to kill a member of my family who I'd just met and actually liked. Thankfully, the ref eventually blew his whistle: we had won the FA Cup.

Later the following week, when Uncle John came back from visiting family in Liverpool, I drove him to the airport. We stopped off for lunch and discussed what had been a momentous trip.

'Why did you leave Liverpool, Uncle John?' I asked.

'I had to get away,' he replied. 'To get away from my mother. It was too claustrophobic.'

People in my family didn't speak like this. But John was so direct. So honest. No phoney sentimentality.

'Me too,' I said.

'But I love going back now', he continued. 'It's good to go back. I live in Australia. My family are there, and I've spent most of my life there. But Liverpool is home.'

I knew what he meant: he'd had to leave to come back. Twenty years before me, Uncle John had done exactly what I'd had to do, but he had found a way back and now he was showing me that not only was it possible, it was essential.

131

15

Heading Home

I DECIDED I wanted to reconnect with my father's side of the family first. He had two brothers still alive, Michael and Gerard. I contacted both and asked if I could visit. I hadn't seen much of them since my dad's funeral in 1978, but they were pleased to hear from me, and we made a date. I wasn't entirely sure what I was going to say to them, though.

Carl Jung once said that when he became a well-known figure, the great and the good wanted to meet him. He added that he'd never had a decent conversation with any of them; all of his best conversations, he claimed, were with strangers on trains. Mine was with a stranger in a car that was booked from a local company, Radcliffe Cars, to pick me up at Lime Street on the day I was to meet my uncles. I sat in the back of the car, feeling very anxious and beginning to regret the whole idea of reconnecting with my family. The driver, a cheerful man in his sixties, introduced himself as Billy Radcliffe and asked where we were going. I gave him my uncle Michael's address and, for some reason, told him that my uncle was recovering from a quintuple bypass.

'Oh, I've had one of them,' said Billy. 'Yeah, tell your uncle he might start feeling a bit depressed in a month or two. I did. I just wanted to cry all the time. So I took myself off to a place where the relatives of the Hillsborough victims met. I thought they'd understand about all that. They were kind enough to let me go along and have a good cry. After a few weeks I felt as right as rain.'

Listening to Billy talk about this most difficult part of his life so generously made me feel much better. His familiar accent, his warmth and his humour touched me and I relaxed. Billy is no longer with us but, thirty years later, whenever I go to an Everton game I still call Radcliffe cars, and Billy's son Michael (even though he's a Liverpool fan) never lets me down.

That day I met Michael first. When I arrived at his house, I could see he was exhausted from the heart operation but happy to see me, and we reminisced for a while about my dad.

My next stop was Uncle Gerard. Within minutes I felt at ease in his company. He was quick-witted, lively and very funny, and he made me laugh like my father had made me laugh.

I felt at home with both of them. They were my family, and I wanted more of them. I called my Uncle Gerard the following week and told him I was going to get season tickets for Everton and asked if he wanted to come. He did.

16

An Evertonian Takes Charge

FOR THE next thirty years I sat next to my Uncle Gerard in the same seats in what became the Brian Labone Lounge. From 1995 until his death in 2013, my stepfather John, also an Everton fan, joined us. 1995 was the last time we had to open the trophy cabinet, which means we acquired our season tickets to coincide with a thirty-year drought at Goodison Park. Do I regret it? Not for a second. When you know you are losing the war, it's vital to enjoy the small victories. And thankfully there have been plenty of small victories.

One of them, however, was not Kendall's third stint as manager, which saw him preside over a second flirtation with relegation in three years. We only managed a draw against Coventry on the final day of the season and stayed in the league due to a better goal difference than Bolton. Kendall left almost immediately. It was a sad end; he was a shadow of his former self. There were stories that his drinking had become a problem, and he admitted as much himself. He had served the club as a brilliant player and our most successful manager, and quite rightly the club named a stand after him after his death in 2015. We should remember him for that.

At that point we were owned by Peter Johnson, a self-confessed Liverpool fan, who had made his fortunes selling Christmas hampers. He would insist on wooing prospective big signings not at the stadium or a flash restaurant in the city but at his Park Foods office in a business park in Birkenhead. Classy. It's said that when we were trying to land the England goalkeeper, Nigel Martyn, Johnson proudly gave him a detailed tour of the hamper-making facility, after which Martyn promptly signed for Leeds.

Johnson was an owner from a different time. He was a local businessman who was wealthy enough to run a club in the old First Division, but the world was changing fast and the Premier League's obsession with money meant that owners like Johnson were becoming extinct. He was a tiny fish in a big shark-infested pond. At one derby game at Anfield, when we were down 3-1, a smartarse on the Kop hoisted a banner that said: 'Well done, agent Johnson. Mission accomplished.'

The fans clamoured for Johnson to buy better players but, in order to balance the books, all he could do was sell our best players. The sale of our popular club captain, Gary Speed, to Newcastle infuriated the fans, but when Duncan Ferguson was sold to Newcastle without the consent of the manager Walter Smith, there was uproar.

By this time, I knew Bill Kenwright was keen to take over the club. On our train journeys up to Liverpool on matchdays, it was clear he was frustrated at how the club was being run. So it was no surprise when, in 1999, Bill rang me to say that he was launching a bid to buy the club from Johnson. He asked me if I would invest. His plan was to get as many of his friends and colleagues to give what they could, alongside a couple of big investors, to form a consortium to take control of the club. And so True Blue Holdings was formed. An Evertonian was now in charge.

We knew that Bill loved the club, but would he have the resources to reverse its fortunes? In 2002 he sacked Walter Smith and replaced him with another Scot, the 38-year-old manager of Preston North End, David Moyes. Moyes had been doing well in the lower leagues, but the big question was whether he would do the business in the top division.

17

Welcome, David Moyes

THAT YEAR was also a significant one for me. I had discovered a lump on the right side of my neck, which eventually was diagnosed in the August as cancer. Surgery followed and I was about to embark on a six-week course of daily radiotherapy. Since becoming a season ticket holder, I had also sponsored one match every season as part of a very important corporate entertainment policy at Hat Trick Productions. Honest. I did it only to further good relations between our company and our wider industry partners. To that end I sponsored games against London teams, and over the years have been joined by Tottenham fans Ade Edmondson and Paul Whitehouse and Arsenal fans Rory McGrath and Clive Anderson.

In October 2002 I was due to take a group of sixteen people to see Everton play Arsenal. The only drawback was that the day of the game was exactly halfway through my radiotherapy. The doctor said I shouldn't go to the game, that I needed to rest, and the common-sense part of my brain also advised me to take it easy, but fortunately I didn't listen to either.

We had hired a coach to take the predominantly Arsenal contingent and me up to Goodison. The bus bubbled with Goonerish banter; understandably they were filled with that sense of entitlement that comes from winning the league and not being beaten for thirty consecutive games. I, on the other hand, wasn't feeling great. The radiotherapy was doing its work, and the dread I was feeling about the coming game wasn't doing much for my fragile immune system. Maybe I should have stayed at home with my meditation tapes and broccoli juice.

The game followed the expected pattern to begin with: Arsenal scored first through that well-known underpants model Freddie Ljungberg in the eighth minute. The inevitable goal rush didn't happen, though, and we scrapped – as all Moyes's teams do – to keep the lead down to one. In the twenty-third minute our centre-forward, Tomasz Radzinski, equalised. But Arsenal continued to dominate and threatened to break down our defence, and we didn't look like scoring.

Then, in the seventy-first minute, Moyes brought on a young man from the Academy, a sixteen-year-old schoolboy from Croxteth who looked like he still played with his mates in the street: Wayne Rooney. Within twenty minutes of coming on, he changed not just the game but the course of his whole life. In the ninetieth minute Rooney brought a high ball down perfectly, turned his powerful frame towards the Stanley Park End, and from about 25 yards he picked his spot and lashed the ball past the England goalkeeper, David Seaman. The boy ran to the touchline, held his arms aloft and roared. We did the same. Clive Tyldesley, the ITV commentator, yelled: 'Remember the name – Wayne Rooney.' In the post-match interview Arsène Wenger said in his usual understated way that Rooney was the best English 'talent' he had seen since he'd been in the country. And he was ours – well, for the time being, but the secret was out.

The coach journey back to London was a quieter affair; it had been a long day and the Gooners had been taught a footballing lesson by a sixteen-year-old

Scouser. I was very happy, but the doctor had been right: this had all been a bit too much. Just as I was settling into my seat for a much-needed snooze, my phone rang. The voice on the other end was familiar but sounded sombre: 'It's Angus.'

It was Angus Deayton, the brilliant host of our long-running hit panel show *Have I Got News for You*. 'They're going to run those stories again.' Angus had been exposed earlier that year in a classic tabloid sting, doing cocaine with a hooker in a Manchester hotel – when he was up there for a game, I suppose. Being born in Surrey, he was of course a Manchester United fan. He had bravely hosted the show that week and been duly mocked by Paul Merton and Ian Hislop, but phoenix-like he seemed to have survived and was still on the show.

'What do you mean, Angus, the same stories?'

'Well… similar… allegations.'

'Oh, you mean similar behaviour just different personnel?'

The following morning Wayne Rooney dominated the back page of the *News of the World* while Angus Deayton took the front. The claims were more lurid and more graphic, and by the end of the following week when Deayton had become a punchline we had to let him go. That was twenty-three years ago. A few years later, the same tabloids who that day heralded the arrival of a young football star onto the world stage would plaster him all over the front pages too. It's what they do.

. . .

My thirty years as a season ticket holder may not have seen us win any silverware, but under Moyes we punched above our weight now and then. In 2005 we finished fourth, one place above Liverpool, which is definitely one of those small victories that give Everton fans so much joy. We would be at the top table next season; they wouldn't. The irony was that Liverpool had just lifted the Champions League, winning on penalties against AC Milan. We couldn't stop laughing.

Unfortunately, we laughed too soon. UEFA could clearly not contemplate the current holders not taking part, so they made a special case for Liverpool to enter the tournament. They created a new rule just for them. Of course, they bloody did.

As if Liverpool gate-crashing our year in Europe through some back-door chicanery wasn't bad enough, worse was yet to come. We were drawn against the classy Spanish team Villareal. It was a tight first leg at Goodison that ended with us taking a 2-1 defeat to Spain. In the return leg, they scored first, making the deficit two goals, then Mikel Arteta curled a beautiful free-kick over the wall and into the Villareal net: 3-2. Minutes later Arteta, again with his precision-tooled right foot, took the perfect corner and landed the ball on the head of our centre-forward, Duncan Ferguson, who obliged by rocketing it in to bring us level.

Only he didn't. The referee, Pierluigi Collina, first pointed to the centre spot but then suddenly swivelled round and, to everyone's surprise, indicated a foul in the six-yard box, awarding Villareal a free-kick. No one – not the players, the crowd or the match commentators – could see an infringement. Later Collina claimed he saw Marcus Bent tug at a Spanish player's jersey. The slow-motion replay tells the opposite story, though: it was Bent who was being impeded by the defender, albeit only slightly. When Ferguson asked the referee why he had given the foul, Collina smiled and cupped his ear as if he couldn't understand what Ferguson was saying. But he was being an arsehole; Collina's English is better than Ferguson's. Three days later Collina retired from being a referee. To my mind, he gave up refereeing that day at Villareal.

•   •   •

My youngest son, Jack, was born in 2004 – just in time to sit on his dad's lap and watch the Euros. My plan was to get him obsessed with football before he could reason. As a toddler he showed an interest in kicking a ball, so as soon as he could walk I began taking him to Goodison. He was too young to know what was happening on the pitch, which was probably a blessing at that point. A couple of years later he was the team mascot and now he is a lifelong Blue. His brother George also became infected with the same virus a few years later, and even their older brother, Joe, who isn't that obsessed with football, said to me a couple of years ago: 'You might like to know I've transferred my almost total lack of interest in Arsenal to my almost total lack of interest in Everton.' It's a great source of pleasure for me to have three sons, all born within shouting distance of Stamford Bridge, become Evertonians. Even on my worst days I can give thanks that I don't have a Chelsea fan under my roof.

In 2008 Jack was too young to travel to Florence to see Everton play Fiorentina in the last sixteen of the

UEFA Cup (now Europa League). I went with my Uncle Gerard, stepfather John and Paul, a young man who worked in the finance department at Hat Trick. We had a lovely time in Florence but the game was a dismal affair. First, the Italian police were unduly aggressive outside the stadium, which created some panic and lot of anger. Then the game itself did not go well. In the pouring rain we lost 2-0.

My abiding memory of that night is the wet walk back from the stadium. Thousands of us were traipsing through the streets of one of the most beautiful cities in the world, and I overheard two Everton fans consoling themselves after the defeat:

'Well, even if we go out, we've had a great time following them around Europe.'

'Yeah, remember that big beer tent in Nurnberg where the ale was half price?'

'Yeah, and Alkmaar was sound. That big, long bar in the town square.'

'Yeah.'

'But Florence, what a shithole!'

'Nowhere decent to get a pint.'

'Yeah.'

I was thinking of getting a T-shirt made with the

words 'Florence: what a shithole' just to commemorate that night.

By the way, we beat the Italian side 2-0 at Goodison, levelling the scores. But don't get too excited – we didn't win. No, that would be out of character. We lost on penalties.

. . .

When Jack was ten I took him to see Everton play Lille in a group game of the 2014 Europa League. We went with an old friend, Paul Roberts, a very successful producer and promoter who I had first met in the 1980s when he put on the stage tour of our Channel 4 show *Who Dares Wins*. Like me, Paul had a son, Joe, who was an obsessed Everton fan. So imagine the moment of utter amazement and wonder for these two young men when the entire Everton squad entered the restaurant of the hotel we were staying in. It was hours before the kick-off, so the team were chilling out. At one point they were shepherded out to take a walk around the grounds and, of course, our two sons followed them. The boys were in dreamland. Watching them watching their heroes was the highlight of the trip. These aren't just the small victories of being a football fan, they are the lasting memories.

The game was a boring 0-0. The French police decided to use tear gas on the Everton fans beforehand, which made for a fetid atmosphere inside the stadium. In the second leg we didn't need tear gas to make the French fans weep. We just hammered them 3-0 and went top of our group. But, rather than motoring on from there, we went out in the knock-out rounds to Dynamo Kiev.

By now I was in a rhythm of going to Liverpool on the train to see the home games, usually in the company of Bill Kenwright and Paul Roberts. In the early days my young daughter, Paige, would come along to visit her Nana June. Paige was obsessed with Paul's hair and treated him rather like a large doll, arranging his hairstyle into weird shapes. I remember him being endlessly patient. She's now thirty-five and still visits Paul and his family. Later Paul and I added our young sons to the trip as soon as they could walk. Over the next fifteen years we watched Joe Roberts and Jack Mulville grow from being little boys into young men. The bonds created by these trips are one of the unforeseen rewards of a commitment to a football team, and I would say they are strengthened when the team is struggling. We had plenty of opportunity to strengthen those bonds after David Moyes left the club in 2013 and we spiralled towards the bottom of the league.

Recommended personally by fellow Scot Alex Ferguson to be his successor at Old Trafford, what could possibly go wrong for Moyes? Sadly, just about everything. The Manchester United squad was ageing and needed rebuilding, and Moyes was not a big international name like José Mourinho or Pep Guardiola, so perhaps the prima donnas in the dressing room didn't take to him. Whatever the reason, Moyes didn't last the season and was sacked after a 2-0 defeat at Goodison Park.

18

The Revolving Door

EVERTON HAD enjoyed eleven years of relative stability and some moderate success under Moyes, who clearly enjoyed a good relationship with Bill Kenwright. Where would the chairman look for his replacement? Enter Roberto Martínez, who to this day can say he is the only football manager to win the FA Cup in the same season that he took his team down to the Championship. He lasted two seasons.

Bill was aware that the club was not properly financed. Other teams in the league were being snapped up by dubious oil billionaires or American businessmen. Bill was one of the last local-lads-made-good to own his boyhood club and he knew he didn't have the financial heft to compete, so he went off and found us our very own billionaire, Farad Moshiri. We were prepared, like all fans, to conveniently ignore any of his disquieting associations away from the club as long as this bloke would spend, spend, spend.

And spend he did. First of all, he appointed that bubbly character Ronald Koeman as manager in June 2017 and then, in October 2017, sacked him. We then had our Sam Allardyce experience. Allardyce saved the patient but the quality of life was poor, and he went a year later. Next came Marco Silva, who is now doing a great job at Fulham but didn't complete his second season with us and was sacked after a 5-2 defeat against Liverpool that left us eighteenth in the table.

Remarkably, Carlo Ancelotti – the five-time Champions League winner – was next through the manager's door. Moshiri had brought the coolest manager in football to Goodison, who in turn brought James Rodríguez, the brilliant Golden Boot-winning Colombian who had played for him at Real Madrid.

We started that season brilliantly, beating Spurs at White Hart Lane 1-0 for the first time since 2008. The link-up play between the skilful Rodríguez, our attacking French left wing-back Lucas Digne, and Dominic Calvert-Lewin, who scored eight goals in the first five matches, saw us top of the league by October. Inevitably, results trailed off and we finished tenth – but not before beating Liverpool 2-0 at Anfield and knocking Mourinho's Spurs out of the FA Cup 5-4. In that game, when we scored the fifth goal the camera cut to Ancelotti and, while the Everton bench went nuts, he simply took another sip of his coffee. Like I said: the coolest manager in football. Sadly, all this excitement took place during Covid so we could only watch it from our bubbles.

Ancelotti was a class act and, if we're honest, we couldn't quite work out what he was doing at Everton. Moshiri had probably offered him a fortune but, even so, Goodison was a far cry from the Bernabéu. So when Real Madrid realised their mistake in letting him go and offered him his old job back, he took it. How could he not? Still, it was a fun year having one of the greats on the touchline.

From the sublime to the ridiculous: Rafa Benítez. The ex-Liverpool manager still lived in Merseyside, so I guess the commute appealed. But come on, this guy once called Everton a small club! Banners appeared in the Gwladys Street end, pointing out that he was not welcome. He never recovered, and when we slipped yet again into the relegation zone he was shown the door and drove back to his house on the Wirral.

19

A Goodison Miracle

FRANK LAMPARD was next in the barrel. Lampard had played for one of the best teams in the league and now here he was managing one of the worst. He had less than three seasons' experience as a manager – one at Derby and eighteen months at his former club, Chelsea – but could he step up to the challenge of turning Everton around?

We struggled in the 2021/22 season and found ourselves needing to beat Crystal Palace in the last home game of the season to secure safety. Due to the eccentric fixture list coming out of Covid, we were scheduled to play them on Thursday 19 May. It was a must-see game. In a perverse way these nail-biting relegation battles were becoming our cup finals, and the atmosphere on these occasions at Goodison was unmissable. But I missed this one.

The Merseyside Youth Association, of which I am a patron, was holding its first gala dinner after Covid. Its inspirational leader, Gill Bainbridge – mindful that Liverpool is football-mad – had scheduled the dinner on a day when football matches never normally take place, Thursday 19 May, but now it was clashing with one of the biggest games of the season. My son George, who was at college in Liverpool, was due to come to the gala with me but when he worked out it clashed with the Palace game he asked to be excused. How could I say no?

The dinner was a great success, though, and I was glad to see that every table was filled. The room was full of both Liverpool and Everton fans. You could tell who the Everton fans were: every five minutes we were discreetly checking the results on our phones under the table. After twenty minutes it was 0-0: so far so good. Then another quick check of the phone: shit, Jean-Philippe Mateta had put Crystal Palace ahead on 21 minutes. We badly needed to win this game. Our last match of the season the following week was away to Arsenal and there was no way we were getting any points there. I tried to concentrate on the gala.

Fifteen minutes later, another sneaky check of the phone: shit! Crystal Palace had scored again. I felt sick. As news of the second Palace goal went round the room, I detected a ripple of both laughter and dread from other guests. No prizes for guessing which noises were coming from which quarter.

After the speeches I went for a pee. There was another man already at the urinal in full flow. Usually peeing at the urinal is a solitary activity; anyone will tell you that eye contact with other users is not encouraged, let alone turning to your neighbour in the next stall and engaging them in conversation. Call me old-fashioned, but there is something uncomfortable about chit-chatting with a stranger when you are holding your penis. Tonight, though, this man didn't care. He needed to share, and I totally understood that need.

'Have you seen the half-time score?' he asked.

How did he know I was an Evertonian? Was there something in my peeing technique that told him I was a man under a great deal of stress?

'Yes,' I replied. 'I can't believe it. We're going down.'

He looked at me in despair and said: '2-0 at half-time. We need a bloody miracle, mate.'

With that he zipped up and left. But then Everton did what Everton do: Michael Keane, our centre-half, pulled one back on fifty-four minutes, Richarlison drew us level on seventy-five minutes and then, with five minutes to go, Calvert-Lewin headed home the third. We had won 3-2 and would live to fight another season.

It added to the celebratory atmosphere of the evening, and even the Liverpool supporters – or most of them – seemed pleased their rivals were staying up. They reasoned that Everton going down would be a disaster for the city and also they would miss beating us twice a year in the derby games.

I saw George after the game back at his student flat. He had obviously been celebrating, and when he saw me he folded me into a massive hug, saying: 'Oh Dad, it was the best night of my life!' Avoiding relegation was the best night of his life? I knew exactly what he meant. Seeing your team pick up a trophy is a thrilling experience, but so is watching the team you love fight back from 2-0 down to win 3-2 and avoid relegation. George said he'd never seen an atmosphere like it at Goodison. He'll remember it forever.

Lampard was rocketed to local-hero status after that result, but the underlying truth was that the squad wasn't good enough and he wasn't the kind of manager who was best equipped to rummage around in the basement of the Premier League. By January the following year, with the team in the relegation zone, he was shown the door and was replaced by Sean Dyche.

20

A Club in Turmoil

WE WERE now not just a team in crisis but a club in turmoil. Bill Kenwright invited me to be his guest at Craven Cottage in Dyche's first season, and I could tell he was not happy with the set-up at Goodison. Yes, he was the titular chairman and to a certain extent could advise the owner, but it was clear that Moshiri, who was an absentee landlord, knew little about Everton and even less about football. Bill's frustration was obvious. He thought he had done the right thing in selling the club to Moshiri and now he knew he'd got it wrong.

The media seem to have a stereotyped view of Sean Dyche. Yes, he talks with a gruff midlands accent, and he had never managed a glamour club, but he struck me as an intelligent, articulate man who had proved that he could guide a team to punch above its weight. He got off to a good start with a 1-0 home win against Arsenal, but the team struggled to climb the table and we left it to the last day – again – to secure safety with a 1-0 win over Bournemouth. We were running on fumes. And then just when you think it couldn't get any worse, it did.

On 17 November 2023, a Premier League disciplinary commission deducted ten points from Everton for a single infringement of the Profitability and Sustainability Rules. The club had apparently exceeded the limit of their expenditure entitlement by £19.5 million. The club appealed on the grounds that it was in fact £9.7 million by their reckoning, and the punishment was reduced to six points.

There was outrage – and not just from Everton fans. There were also politicians who had for some time wondered out loud whether the Premier League was capable of self-governing. When it was pointed out that it looked as though big clubs in the league – like Manchester City, who had been under investigation for 115 infringements – were being treated differently, Richard Masters, the CEO of the Premier League, famously said: 'The standard directions [on the Profitability and

Sustainability Rules] are for everybody, they're not just for the small clubs.'

The atmosphere at Goodison at the next home match, against Manchester United, after this deduction was boiling. The crowd held aloft specially made cards saying, 'Premier League – Corrupt'. We had dropped from mid-table security to the relegation zone overnight. We lost that game 3-0, and yet again there was a sinking feeling that we might go down. The bookies agreed.

But then came another miracle: we went on a four-match run of consecutive wins against Nottingham Forest, Newcastle, Chelsea and Burnley, clawing our way out of the relegation zone. This monumental achievement confirmed in my mind that Sean Dyche was the right man at the right time. It also gave birth to a new Everton song on the terraces. To the tune of 'She'll Be Coming Round the Mountain', we sang: 'You can stick your points deduction up your arse!'

We finished the season relatively comfortably, in fifteenth place, but by this time Moshiri was keen to get the club off his hands. And we couldn't wait for that to happen.

For a while we held our breath while the owner dangled Everton in front of a Miami-based private investment company, 777. Their founder, Josh Wander, would attend games in a baseball cap and sunglasses, looking like an extra in *Succession*. They owned other clubs across the world, whose fans regularly protested at the way their club was being run. Thankfully for us, the deal collapsed when they couldn't complete in time. It felt like a lucky escape.

21

A New Beginning

SEAN DYCHE had defied gravity for two seasons and kept us up against the odds, for which every Everton fan should be eternally grateful. Yes, I know he plays a certain type of football but, given the quality of the squad, he performed miracles. Sam Allardyce was once asked why his teams didn't play in the same manner as Pep Guardiola's teams. He replied: 'If I had Kevin De Bruyne in my team, I'd play like Manchester City. But I haven't, so I don't.'

Managers like Allardyce and Dyche may be the workhorses of the Premier League, dragging their burdens around the lowlands of the table, but they are a vital part of that ecosystem as much as the glamorous show ponies prancing around higher up. Having said that, I couldn't wait for new owners to come in and reboot the whole club, and if that meant appointing a new manager, it would be a case of 'thanks, Sean, see you later.'

My wish was granted in December 2024, when The Friedkin Group, a serious player in both the sports and media world, finally bought the club and ended the uncertainty. The following month, with the club just one point above the relegation zone, it was announced that Dyche would be leaving. Speculation about his possible replacement began immediately – perhaps some bright wunderkind from one of the European leagues? This was an exciting moment; we were heading into a new future.

And then, two days after Dyche's departure, it was announced that David Moyes would be the next Everton manager. Where was my male-model, thirty-something tactical genius with a German accent? Moyes had done a great job for us given his restrictions, and he been treated unfairly by Manchester United when he left us in 2013, but since then he had been sacked by Real Sociedad after a year, hadn't been able to prevent Sunderland from going down in 2017, and then had two stints at West Ham (where, to be fair, he did win the Europa Conference League, whatever the hell that is). I wasn't convinced he would do much better than his predecessor.

I was wrong. In his first eight games we picked up fifteen points and were safely nestled just below the halfway mark in the league. Moyes's job was to keep us up so we could sit at the top table when we took possession of our new stadium in August 2025. By the time we played our last Premier League match at Goodison Park he had done that with ease. By the end of the season, we were showing top-four form.

Moyes had clearly returned to Everton with a purpose. They say for a certain personality type, the desire to prove people wrong is a powerful driver of ambition. I wonder if somewhere in Moyes's consciousness is the desire to prove Manchester United wrong. I hope so.

We now had a new owner, a new manager and a new stadium. The next time I would watch the team would be on the banks of the Royal Blue Mersey!

22

Moving Home

23 AUGUST 2025: the date of our first home game in the new stadium. George and I take the usual train to Liverpool, but at Lime Street Station our normal routine changes. This time we take a taxi not to Walton but to the Hill Dickinson Stadium. It doesn't trip off the tongue, I know, but at least Hill Dickinson, a commercial law firm, was founded in Liverpool in 1810 and isn't a Middle Eastern airline.

Our first view of the stadium is impressive as it looms large on the Bramley-Moore Dock, once the dropping-off point for ships from around the world. We find our turnstile and show our virtual tickets on our phones. I recognise a couple of former Goodison staff, and they recognise us. Smiles and handshakes.

It's a nice moment. Familiar. But this is all so strange, so different. We take the lift to the second floor. It feels like I'm at an away game.

We walk into the lounge where we will have some food before the game, and there on the next table are Debbie and Larry with their two sons, Pete and Gary. The family who had sat next to us at Goodison for many years, and who I was convinced I wouldn't see again, are there in front of me. None of us can believe it. I hug them like we're survivors of some natural disaster.

We admit that we're a little nervous – not just about the game but about the change of routine. We all had a muscle memory of getting to Goodison, sitting in those familiar seats for thirty years, greeting regular members of staff every home game. After years of self-imposed exile from Goodison in the 1970s and 80s, for these last thirty years going there had become part of my life. We even had a family reunion in one of the Goodison hospitality suites. When my stepfather died, we had his wake there, and later my mum's too – and she wasn't even an Everton fan. I remember all the games Hat Trick sponsored at Goodison, and the time we voted young Wayne Rooney Man of the Match because we all wanted to meet him. I remember Dot and Debbie, who looked after the sponsor's lounge and who I knew hadn't been transferred to the new place.

George and I sit in our seats for that first league game against Brighton and look around our new football home. It is an amazing sight. To our right behind the goal is a vast, steep bank of seats that will no doubt take the place of the old Gwladys Street end and from where a lot of the noise will come. I read that the maximum angle of any such seating is 35 degrees. Our seating is 34.99 degrees; the intention is to create a steep cauldron-shaped bowl to intensify the atmosphere.

A new stadium had been the twinkle in Bill Kenwright's eye ever since he took over the club in the late 1990s. After a couple of failed attempts, permission was given in 2017 to build on the Bramley-Moore Dock. Bill died in 2023, and in the last year of his life he was a notable absence from Goodison. Due to the anger displayed by the fans at the way the club was being run, many of the board decided to stay away. Bill was the chairman but by now was not in control of the club. Above all else, though, he was a fan. He never lived to sit in this stadium but I would hope that the new owners might at some point name a part of it after him to acknowledge his role in the club's history and the establishment of this new state-of-the-art stadium. Or perhaps the council might rename one of the streets leading up to the ground. It's the least we could do.

George and I sit in very comfortably padded seats. At one point my backside and lower back become quite hot. Am I having a stroke? Have I wet myself? On further investigation, I discover I have inadvertently turned on a switch that heats the seat. Panic over. That will be nice in January, but on a hot day in August?

The game ends with us beating Brighton 2-0. We all agree it's good to start the new era with a win. The additions of Jack Grealish and Kiernan Dewsbury-Hall look promising, and we leave with a spring in our step. It's been a great day.

I tell George that he and his brothers will be coming here when they are my age, and this will be the stadium where he will bring his children. It occurs to me that when we left our family home in 2010 we all cried, and the children wrote notes to the next family and buried them in a tin in the garden. It was a sad day, but about a month later I noticed I was driving past our old house and I felt nothing. It was just a house, not our home any more. Our home is where the people we love live. And so it was for me and Goodison: I love

Everton Football Club, and wherever Everton is will be my football home.

I have supported this club for sixty-five years, taken first by my father. Then I ran away to university in the south and I either couldn't or wouldn't go back until, after a chance conversation with Bill Kenwright, I began a slow return. The snap decision to buy a season ticket in 1995 opened the door and brought me closer to my family, and being closer to my family helped me rediscover the city that formed me.

I am now very involved with setting up a free school for 16–18-year-olds to learn all the skills to get good jobs in the creative industries. It's in the iconic Littlewoods Pools Building, which was owned by a former Everton chairman and director John Moores. The plan is to turn this magnificent space into a state-of-the-art studio and production centre with a school sitting in the middle of it. I'm also part of Imagine Liverpool, an advisory group to support the regeneration of the parts of the city that still need it. I am up and down to Lime Street on a regular basis these days and, when I get off the train and hear the seagulls and that beautiful Scouse accent, I breathe out: I'm home.

Liverpool is a fantastic city, filled with extraordinary, creative and generous people. It is a city fuelled by love and a heady mix of resilience, humour and belligerence. I'm sad that I couldn't see that when I left in 1974. I had to go away, have some adventures, make some terrible choices, then some better ones, and finally come back with a new pair of glasses to see my family and my city clearly for what seemed like the first time.

Everton FC played a huge part in that journey, and for that I will always be grateful.

Acknowledgements

I WOULD like to acknowledge some people who have helped me with this book and others who have supported me over the years. I would like to thank Ian Ridley for suggesting I write this book and encouraging me to finish it. Charlotte Atyeo, who improved upon the original with her smart and intelligent insights. The team at Floodlit Dreams for all their support in launching this book. My friend Tim Mellors, without whom I wouldn't be here. And Bruce Lloyd, the Welsh wizard who made me see straight and face some painful truths. Bill Kenwright, who guided me back to Goodison. My uncle Gerard for the last thirty years of watching games together. My wonderful children, Paige, Joe, George and Jack, who have all shared with me this Everton journey in their own way. Finally and most importantly my extraordinary wife, Karen, who – to quote Jack Nicholson in *As Good As It Gets* – 'made me want to be a better man.'

ALSO IN THE
FOOTBALL SHORTS SERIES

Pantomime Hero
Jimmy Armfield
*Memories of the man who
lifted Leeds after Brian Clough*
By Ian Ridley

The Homecoming
The Lionesses and Beyond
By Jane Purdon

Blue was the Colour
A Tale of Tarnished Love
By Andy Hamilton

Double Acts
*A Modern History of Tottenham
in 10½ Strike Partnerships*
By Julie Welch

Namaste, Geezer
Life as a Fan and Journalist
of Asian Heritage
By Shekhar Bhatia

Excerpts from a new England
Gareth Southgate:
Eight years and Eighteen Episodes
By David Winner

www.floodlitdreams.com